"Jason Brown's work has always had some of the allure of the coast of Maine—vivid and frightening and beautiful. I read his books for the beautiful, amber sense of humor mixed with a lyrical sense of melancholy and fate. *Character Witness* has all these literary pleasures, along with the pace and tension of a thriller. . . . A gorgeous and harrowing book."

—Tom Beller, author of *Lost in the Game*

"What love can remain in a mother-son relationship shaped by her severe mental illness, substance addiction, chaos, lies, and unforgivable transgressions of abuse? The answer is *Character Witness*, an astonishing masterwork of memoir. Writing with electric intelligence, heartbreaking candor, and deeply moving insight, Jason Brown allows his reader to understand the seemingly impossible: the unspeakable traumas and complications of intergenerational abuse, and how, once spoken, a new life for a family may be possible."

—Megan Harlan, author of *Mobile Home: A Memoir in Essays*

"Just start with the first sentence: You won't be able to stop. *Character Witness* reads like a fever dream. It is a Denis Johnson short story come to life. You feel for his mom; you want Jason to escape: 'this cannot continue; how can it change?' And then the next page happens. Brown's work is consistently fearless, he doesn't blink, can't stop turning situations over in his head. He is a marvelous writer. The last third of this memoir is almost painful in its beauty and the purity of its love."

—Charles Bock, author of *I Will Do Better* and *Beautiful Children*

"Jason Brown has a deep, touching, and fresh insight into the abiding attachment and love that family both gives us and subjects us to. Anyone not from a 'perfect' family—that is, anyone—will recognize the stumbles and pitfalls and small triumphs that chart the course of family life. The story proceeds relentlessly, but with a light touch even in its darkest moments. It is told in clear, vivid prose, without affectation or false bravado. . . . *Character Witness* will stand with the best modern American memoirs."

—**Tobias Wolff**, author of *This Boy's Life: A Memoir* and *Our Story Begins: New and Selected Stories*

Character Witness

American Lives | Series editor: Tobias Wolff

Character Witness

A Memoir

JASON BROWN

University of Nebraska Press | Lincoln

The University of Nebraska Press is part of a land-grant institution with campuses and programs on the past, present, and future homelands of the Pawnee, Ponca, Otoe-Missouria, Omaha, Dakota, Lakota, Kaw, Cheyenne, and Arapaho Peoples, as well as those of the relocated Ho-Chunk, Sac and Fox, and Iowa Peoples.

♾️

For customers in the EU with safety/GPSR concerns, contact:
gpsr@mare-nostrum.co.uk
Mare Nostrum Group BV
Mauritskade 21D
1091 GC Amsterdam
The Netherlands

Library of Congress Control Number: 2025007072

Set in Minion Pro by A. Shahan.

For Isabella, Nicola, Susan

Character Witness

Prologue   THE WRONG JASON BROWN

I was driving back from running an Alcoholics Anonymous meeting at a prison in Orange, New York, when blue lights appeared in my rearview mirror. I had gone through a rural intersection and taken a right onto a narrow road. I might have rolled through the stop sign. I took off my seat belt so I could dig through the glove compartment for my paperwork. After years of driving illegally, I now had a license, registration, and insurance. The officer approached. I rolled my window down and placed my hands on the steering wheel. A young guy around my age, mid-twenties, with the same kind of pizza-dough face as mine, asked me for my documents. Hoping for a warning, I handed over my information, and he returned to his cruiser.

I went back to staring out the windshield and thinking about a poet in my graduate program I thought I was in love with, who wisely saw me as trouble. The light had just started to fade in the tall oaks and maples. When I checked the rearview mirror again, I counted five police cars with twice that many officers gathered nearby in a huddle. One of them spoke on a radio and relayed information to the others. I stopped breathing, and every time one of the cops glanced in my direction, the muscles in my neck ratcheted tighter.

The prison, called the Monterey Shock Incarceration Facility, was where young offenders, almost all of them Black or Hispanic and from New York City, marched around a military-style campus wearing olive-green fatigues, some of them carrying eight-foot logs, while the guards, all white, barked orders. Then the young men sat in neat rows in a cinder-block room and looked at my friend and me, two white guys from a college town who had come to share our "experience, strength, and hope."

This was how it had started for them, I thought now: waiting to be surrounded. Except this couldn't be happening to me, because I was Jason Brown—I was innocent. One of the officers produced a bullhorn, while a half-dozen others approached my car in a crouch, their hands on their guns. From what I could see, the remaining officers seemed to be taking up positions behind the cruisers and preparing for battle.

The officer with the bullhorn raised it to his mouth and said, "Jason Brown, get out of the car with your hands in the air."

They split into two columns, one on either side of my car. Though I knew I should follow the orders of the officer with the bullhorn, I no longer had any control over my arms and legs. My thoughts spun out of my head and flew into the air, leaving my body behind. I felt as if I were watching a TV show about someone named Jason Brown who was about to be arrested for crimes he claimed not to have committed. The Jason Brown in the car was starting to hyperventilate, while the Jason Brown watching this on TV was curious to see what happened next. The approaching officers froze, and the voice through the bullhorn repeated its demand. Either I would step out of the car, or they would drag me out. I understood that if they dragged me out they would be angry, yet I was no more willing to open the door than I would be to shove my hand into the mouth of a shark.

The guy with the bullhorn told everyone to hold on. I sat with my hands molded to the steering wheel. One of the officers ran back to the cruisers. After a minute, the rest of them joined him. Another minute passed. The officer who had originally pulled me over approached my car. He tapped on the roof, handed my license back, and looked around the interior.

"We had the wrong Jason Brown," he said. "There's another Jason Brown with an arrest warrant. He's very dangerous."

My forehead collapsed against the steering wheel. When I eventually leaned back, the officer held a yellow sheet of paper in front of my face.

"What's that?" I said.

"A citation for not wearing your seat belt."

*

To me the name Jason Brown had always sounded like an amateur golfer. In the 1980s and '90s, a spate of future athletes were born with the name Jason, including Jason Brown the professional football player and Jason Brown the figure skater. Another Jason Brown, born two years after me, became a fugitive wanted for murder, in Phoenix, and appeared on the FBI's Ten Most Wanted list. That Jason Brown was born in California, which I was not. He had a master's degree in international business, which I did not. For a while, he was a Mormon and owned a business called Toys Unlimited. At one point, Jason Brown took a firearms class; at another point, a man claimed that Brown had accidentally shot his truck. A little while later, he allegedly shot an armored-truck driver five times in the head and made off with fifty-six thousand dollars in cash. He hasn't been seen since.

*

I wish I could tell it straight through, but that has never worked out. Too many pills, too much booze, born missing a beat or a bearing—often I come to the end of a sentence not knowing where I started. In graduate school, I started reading Camus, Arendt, Baldwin, many others, but I always came back to Camus, looking for a road map I could recognize. I could go a week, sometimes a month, and I felt almost engaged, motivated, invested. Then, without warning, I was frozen. The muffled voices of my family on the phone, fellow students, and others seemed to come from down the street. For long stretches of time, I couldn't move.

"Well, you were born late," my mother had once told me, "and before I even laid eyes on you, the doctor told me that you looked like a Neanderthal. I didn't think that was such a nice thing to say. We couldn't separate you from your bottle for at least four years, until you developed trench mouth, and when we brought you to preschool you curled up in the corner and moaned until the teachers made me come back for you. Also, for a long time, you would only play with orange toy cars, and then, one day, you found your father's hammer and smashed all your cars to pieces."

✳

Like teenagers from any generation, I suppose, my friends and I wanted everything destroyed and remade in our image. We were the last generation for whom there were no rules. Pretending to be undercover police, Dan and I borrowed a friend's blue Chevy, put a flashing light on the dash, and pulled people over. Once, when I picked up a job crewing on a sailboat going from Florida to Maine, I left school for three weeks and told everyone my godmother had died in a plane crash. I was going to Florida to sprinkle her remains over a coral reef. I told kids that I was from a rich family and even had them drop me off in other neighborhoods, only to have to hike halfway across town to my house.

Already drunk and driving with a guy from my high school whom I didn't know very well, I stopped at a 7-Eleven to buy beer. After we loaded the back of the car, everything went dark until sometime later, when I came to naked in a one-room cabin. I was lying on my back, and a woman I had never met was sitting on top of me. Apparently, we were having sex. A dozen or more people sat drinking in the cabin. "Who are you?" I asked. Her eyes were closed.

In my last year of high school, my father moved out and my friend Tom moved in with me. My parents' house in Portland, Maine, had a windowless, dank basement apartment where Tom and I lived.

"You know, he's very, very handsome," my mother said one morning, while I was pouring myself a bowl of cereal upstairs. I supposed there wasn't much I could do about that. There were handsome people out there. That I might be one of them, as my mother had said many times, in no way canceled out the existence of other handsome people and of the desires that ripped through our lives like the wind. My mother blushed, as if she were fifteen. She put her hand on my arm, smiled, and raised her eyebrows. I poured my cereal into the sink.

In the spring, a month before we graduated, my mother, Tom, and I were drinking in the kitchen when we ran out of beer. I took Tom's car to get more from the corner store. The name on my fake ID was Bob. Bob Brown. On the way back, I crashed into a fire hydrant and slammed my forehead into the windshield. The car wouldn't start, so I left it there and walked home with the beer under my arm. It was dark by the time I reached the house. I sat at the kitchen table as blood dripped down my cheek, along my neck, and into my shirt.

"What happened to you?" my mother asked. Tom took a beer out of the case, and she looked at him the same way she looked at me. Or she looked at me the same way she looked at him. He looked at the floor.

At the end of the week, Tom and I were buying a slice of pizza downtown on Exchange Street. We only had enough money for one slice and were trying to split it evenly in half as we stood in an alley.

"Your mom asked me to have sex with her," he said and shrugged. This wouldn't have been an unusual thing to say. Not for us, not in our world. He was just keeping me informed. I waited for him to say more, but he didn't have to. Sex was not something we could say no to. It was all around us. My mother shared whatever sexual thoughts passed through her mind.

Maybe the context started when I was ten. That's the age that started to make sense from other proximate evidence surrounding my memory of getting out of the tub and turning to my mother, who held a towel. Instead of handing it to me, she dried me off: first my head, then my chest, then below. I turned in a circle in front of her. She said, "You're big down there."

It would've been helpful, in a way, if there had been one particularly heinous act I could point to—one act, that is, that stood out from moments like that one, in which I stood next to the bath and she smiled as her hand lingered on me. The same smile, coy and embarrassed, that she would flash in the future when she would come into the bathroom to dry me off, or touch my arm as I passed her in the kitchen, or told me about the men she liked and why.

The same smile she would later offer Tom, my other friends, other men, me.

For Tom and me, our mothers' sexuality was like the coastal fog of our native state: everywhere, in our lungs, slowly suffocating us, though we didn't know we were suffocating. We didn't know what was happening to us when it was happening to us. Even years later we didn't know what we remembered. A person's hand on your body is like a word. It has no meaning—doesn't even exist—outside of context. Once the context is set, once the fog settles in, anyone's hand on my body would feel like her hand. Every woman who ever smiled at me with desire was my mother. If I was drunk or had just met a woman, there was a chance I could make it work, but not for long.

"To those who despair of everything, not reason but only passion can provide a faith, and in this particular case it must be the same passion that lay at the root of the despair—namely, humiliation and hatred." Camus.

*

In college, while blacked out, I took off all my clothes and walked across campus to a party where I started talking in a soft, serious voice about certain key passages in Nietzsche's "The Gay Science." I had blackouts all the time now. Many of them were not really drinking blackouts. I would lie down and fall asleep after a few beers, only to wake up sometime later as someone else. This other Jason Brown liked to be on the move. One night I threw my clothes and furniture out the window. I woke up in the bushes; I woke up in hallways. Once I was down by the Androscoggin River and found a pair of pants hanging from a branch, the name Jason Brown written on the tag.

*

When I was offered my first teaching job at the University of Arizona in Tucson, I couldn't believe that I was going to be living a few miles from my mother. I had gone to graduate school in part to escape from her; now fate was setting me down back in her domain. As

I rolled into Tucson and saw my mother's car parked outside my new rental, I had the feeling that nothing had changed. I had been awarded a prestigious fellowship, published a book, convinced a university to hire me, but beneath the surface, in a deeper current, I was the same. I couldn't make a relationship work, I didn't understand why I felt so distant from people.

When I had a break from teaching, I convinced my new insurance to pay for a five-day codependency workshop at the Caron Foundation, in Pennsylvania. A number of people from AA had attended, and they spoke highly of the ability of the therapists there to take you back to the origin of your damage. By the time I arrived at the orientation, I was sure I had made a huge mistake.

The program was designed for people who were still having trouble with relationships. Most of the people there were in AA. Our group of twenty was mixed in gender and appeared to range in age from sixteen to sixty. After we got to know one another, we broke into small groups of five or six to talk in therapist-guided sessions about the problems, most of them sexual in nature, which had led us there. Then we were handed foam bats to wield against furniture, the floor, walls—anything but the other participants. We were supposed to expunge our rage. That was the plan, I was told.

The food was great, and the therapy didn't work at all. I sat in a circle on the floor with my small group and narrated what I knew about what had happened between my mother and me—a part of my life I had never talked about before, not like this. I wasn't describing anything I had somehow repressed or forgotten, but in telling it to all these strangers, I felt as if I were talking about someone else's life. That person, the person in my story, didn't have anything to do with me.

When I finished, I took up the foam bat and pounded on the chairs and tables and walls while the strangers observed. It was satisfying to beat on objects while the strangers (two of whom, a teenage girl and a forty-two-year-old wife and mother of three, I found attractive) watched me pretend to lapse into a rage storm. For their benefit, I contorted my face and clenched my fists. I grunted. I wanted to be a sensitive but explosive Jason Brown. Misunderstood, sexy—the James Dean of damaged lovers. I had worn my tight black shirt for the occasion. But I wasn't enraged, not in the slightest. When, at age twelve, I had put my fist through the windshield of our car, I was full of rage. When, during my first year of sobriety, I picked up Dan and threw him across the room, I was enraged. I knew I was supposed to get back there now, but I couldn't, not while I was working the audience.

Having relinquished my bat, I returned to the group, curled up into the fetal position, and pretended to cry. I hadn't been told that this was expected, but I understood the script. The mother of three rested her head against my back while the teenager pressed her warm lips against my ear.

Later, in a private meeting with the therapist, I confessed that I didn't think I was supposed to be there. I was a fake. In the same way I had faked my rage in front of the group, I had faked everything else in my life. Starting when I was twelve, I had spent years guzzling booze in a periodic way, but I didn't think I was really an alcoholic. I went to the meetings because I needed somewhere to go. I needed someone to be and *alcoholic* fit better than anything else.

"It's not like anything *happened* to me," I said. Nothing, I meant, that justified how I felt, years after giving up drugs and alcohol. In other words, my mother hadn't had sex with me, so I didn't see what I had to complain about. I was sick of my failed relationships and of how I felt, but, mostly, I was sick of hearing myself complain—yet here I was, complaining again. The more we talked, the more he nodded. I imagined that he could see that I was terrified of myself. I had tried to halt for good all thought, desire, rage—everything— once by slicing up my arms (something I hadn't remembered until recently) and once by throwing myself in front of a bus.

Then the therapist used the word I couldn't apply to my experi- ence with my mother. No one had ever said this word to me, about me. He used the word again together with the words "emotional" and "covert." According to the therapist, all three groupings—the word "incest" alone and the word paired with the other two words—

described what had happened to me, which I found impossible to believe.

I have the ability, always have, of not being wherever it is that I am. I see, I hear, but I am not there, anywhere. This was the case for me now as he explained how my personal context overlapped with the diagnostic context. On one level, these were all just words, like the words of my name. The therapist finished his discussion of my new context and asked me what I thought.

I told him I had no idea. I didn't think anything.

He leaned forward. He had a perfectly manicured, dark-brown beard that matched his eyes. "I don't think that's true," he said.

"But nothing *happened*," I said. "She didn't . . ."

"Didn't what?" he said.

"Do anything to me."

"She did," he said calmly. "Based on what you've described since you got here, she did."

The therapist thought I was trying to avoid the truth, but that wasn't the case. I'd heard other words and acronyms: ADHD, dyslexia, bipolar disorder, alcohol-use disorder, major depressive disorder, generalized anxiety disorder, suicidal ideation—not a disorder but a symptom. Abuse. Survivor. For my mother, what they used to call borderline personality disorder. Maybe we had been winged by some of these, I told myself—my family tree on her side was riddled with examples—but I was no hard case. I knew how these things went. First came the category that only half fit. Categories like footprints in a field. Our lives poured passively into the molds. Then the narrative to support the category. Then more medication that would make me feel less like me than the booze and drugs I had taken to medicate myself in the first place.

The bearded therapist with coffee breath didn't understand that part of me wanted to believe what he had said. If I could accept his word—if I could only agree that something had *happened* to me—then my life would no longer be my fault. Not just parts of my life, certain mistakes, but the whole thing. That was the promise as I saw it. What an incredible relief that would be. The trouble was that I resisted the tools that psychology and academics had given me to explain everything: by absorbing statistics and micro-categorizations of pathologies, traits, and isms, my feelings had become a function of systems, diseases, genetics, class, race, gender. Even if I could put a name to what felt like my true story, it might not be true at all. It might just be the story that made me feel better. I had a sense that there was a disturbing parallel between my desire to obliterate the pain and confusion of my experience with booze and drugs and my desire to extinguish my uncertainty with the totality of interpretation. Maybe both were ways of trying to make the real story disappear.

I left the therapist's office with his words lodged in my brain. A handful of words to describe what was wrong. No words can bear that burden—but when you're drowning and words are all you've got, then words are better than nothing.

Over supper that night, I sat across from the mother of three, just the two of us, not talking, looking at each other between bites. When your context is set early on, you don't feel attracted to the people you are allowed to be attracted to. Only the people you are forbidden from touching can break the spell. I said I was going to the bathroom and slipped out the back of the cafeteria. When I reached my dormitory, I found the teenage girl standing in the hall outside my door. Her room was just around the corner. She hadn't noticed me until my performance, until my fake rage and grief. Now she noticed me. I recognized the look on her face when she raised her chin. Her cheeks were burning, eyes watering. The heat of her sorrow passed right into me, and I understood that she didn't want to talk or play with foam bats. We'd done enough pretending. I shook my head, rushed into my room, shut the door behind me, and turned the lock. Now I was feeling something. Terrified of my bottled-up desire and the certainty that I would always be alone, I stood sobbing at the window and looked out toward the dark woods.

Camus again: "A man who says no, but whose refusal does not imply a renunciation. He is also a man who says yes, from the moment he makes his first gesture of rebellion. . . . He means, for example, that 'this has been going on too long,' 'up to this point yes, beyond it no. . . .' In other words, his no affirms the existence of a borderline."

*

When one becomes the sexual object of one's parent—or, I imagine, of any member of the close family—there is a part of oneself that becomes sealed off like an insect in amber. Over time, one begins to suspect—especially during important moments in relationships, at work, with friends and family—that one is not fully present, not wholly there. Finally, it is impossible to avoid the feeling that this sealed-off part is the real self and therefore the source of all our fear and all our desire. Then it becomes impossible not to feel that this part of us we cannot touch, cannot know, determines who we are and how we see the world. It explains, maybe, why other people never seemed quite real. This explains why when I met people I often had the strange feeling that I was them and not me. Then they walked away, back into their own lives.

*

A local woman found my mother's father where he had killed himself, in the garage attached to the barn, in New Hampshire, in 1996. He had pulled his car inside, connected a hose from the tailpipe to the interior, and gassed himself. Assuming, as people do, that his pet would not want to go on without him, he died with his cat, which had been a present from my mother. They died listening to the rumble of the engine of the car.

One of his daughters (my aunt) disappeared—I have no idea what happened to her. One son later served time in Sing Sing for molesting a boy. His brother, when he was about fifteen, supposedly chased his father through the house while blowing holes in the walls with a gun. He was trying to kill his father but was too drunk to aim. I don't know what happened back there, in that family, not exactly. History is a thunderhead passing over the earth. We are the lightning that touches the ground.

*

In 1991 I lived in Portland, Maine, in a condemned apartment next to a sex shop and across from the Nu Body Health Spa, a place that had nothing to do with anyone's health. I lived with Dan, and we were both three months sober. Behind the apartment was a funeral home. Frequently smoke poured from its smokestacks. One day, a voice told Dan he was Jesus. I asked him if he believed the voice, and he said that at first he did but then he thought about it. I suggested he write a note to himself, *I am not Jesus*, and leave it next to his bed.

It was a Saturday in May, and I wanted Dan to go with me to some kind of gathering. Maybe with AA people at Denny's, I can't remember. I never wanted to go anywhere by myself. I was lucky when I rolled with other people, especially with Dan.

He said he was busy with his old girlfriend. What happened next didn't happen, not in the usual sense. I only know what happened because Dan later told me about it. I lost time as completely as if I had blacked out from downing a fifth. Dan and I weighed about the same—between a hundred and ninety and two hundred pounds—but he was twice as strong as me from lifting weights. Also, he knew how to fight and I didn't, not really. I lifted him off the floor and threw him against the wall. Then I jumped on his chest and tried to strangle him. He got off a good shot to my face at some point. When I came to—when I came back to myself—I tumbled off him, and he scrambled into the corner.

Unremembered acts that we learn about through someone else's report seem to belong to a second self that lives slightly out of reach. Scenes from a novel we read years ago. Sometimes it seems as if we remember what we do before we do it, and our actions feel like the shadow of memory.

*

I went to the Caron Foundation in part because I often had the feeling that I was living in multiple times and multiple places at once. More in my mother's life than in my own. She had spared me the worst of what happened to her—I knew that—but I didn't know how. I couldn't say that either of us had changed. I didn't know of anyone who underwent fundamental changes because they wanted to. Maybe, I thought, it was possible to change, but not without becoming someone you didn't know.

Our mothers were the first people we knew, at first the only ones we could trust, our only gateway to ourselves. If my mother didn't recognize me, I would see myself vanish by becoming a stranger to her.

*

In Tucson, my mother usually couldn't figure out how to make the internet work in her place south of the city. Usually, the answer was that she had not paid the bill. When she called on the phone I had bought her, usually I didn't answer. When I talked to people about my mother, I often lamented the burden of looking after a lost cause. I liked to tell people that she couldn't live without me, but I had already begun to suspect that I couldn't survive without her.

My mother had her own lost causes: cats with terminal diseases, former show dogs abandoned in shelters, her boyfriend from the bus riders' union who slept in a riverbed and complained that the coyotes came at night to nibble on his toes. He saved half his supper from the shelter and gave it to them so they would stop chewing on him. "This probably was not the best idea," my mother said, raising her eyebrows.

She often drove out into the desert south of Tucson with the Samaritans to leave jugs of water at key points for people who had been abandoned by another kind of coyote. More than once, I saw her cruise by in the passenger seat of a white Toyota truck with a fist painted on the door. She wanted to rescue people—"the people with dark hair," as she called them—from history. One jug of water at a time, she would be their savior.

I thought of the men at the Monterey Shock Incarceration Facility, in Orange, New York, years before. Most of the men had been under twenty-five, strong, tall, many of them handsome. They sat upright in their fatigues and looked at us. My friend and I always left the camp feeling as if we had helped those who needed it—those who had been forsaken by history—but I later discovered that we had the story upside down. They were dealers and kingpins, not addicts. They came to our meetings because they were forced to by a world that had given them few if any options. We came to them hoping to be saved from ourselves.

Camus: "Here ends Prometheus' surprising itinerary. Proclaiming his hatred of the gods and his love of mankind, he turns away from Zeus with scorn and approaches mortal men to lead them in an assault against the heavens."

＊

I had a memory that felt more like a dream: I was young, I couldn't remember how young, and I rose from my bed before dawn and walked to the bathroom as if I was being led by someone's hand. I stood on the tub to reach the upper cabinet, took out one of my father's razors, and cut red lines lengthwise along my arms.

When I first stopped drinking, I had a recurring dream that my mother and I were walking through a narrow tunnel that traveled deep underground. We were being led by men with automatic weapons. The air was heavy, hard to breathe, and finally we came to a small room carved out of the earth. The room was lit by a torch, and at the center of the room, on a pedestal, sat a clay bust of a dog's head. The bust radiated an oppressive power that forced me to my knees, and I had to look away. Then I couldn't breathe.

It was only by applying a kind of constant pressure, as a compress is applied to a wound to staunch the bleeding, that I could keep from drifting away, even as it was impossible to say what I was drifting away from.

＊

At the Caron Foundation, I lay in bed at night after the therapy sessions had ended and tried to figure out what to do with the fragments I'd picked up from my mother's stories—handfuls of puzzle pieces dropped from a box. After divorcing my mother's father, my grandmother remarried her high school sweetheart in Buffalo. A few times a year, my mother's father, a traveling salesman, drove over from New Hampshire in an ocean-blue car and took my mother back to the old farm in North Sutton. Because I had been to the farm and knew the smell of must from the stone cellar rising through gaps in the pine floors and knew the sight of crumbling horsehair plaster and the shotgun in the closet—because I had woken in the morning to stare out the warped panes at the lower field dotted with cows and descended the stairs to the kitchen to find my grandfather already drinking—I could see my mother, aged eleven, walking in the winter field below the house with her hands brushing through the air over dry grass.

I was going over a story, looking for what was missing so I didn't have to see what was there. Her thin legs. She held herself taut, arms out to the side, and turned around. The cold dampness on her cheeks anticipated the storm. The limbs of the apple and maple trees bending in the wind. A knotted cloud grew closer as she climbed the front steps and let the porch door slam with a crack. The front hall steeped in a century of wood smoke. Her father passed out on the sofa in the parlor. Her upstairs room remained unchanged. Across the hall, what had been her father's room was also unchanged. A skin of dust covered every piece of furniture.

She woke in the middle of the night and gazed out the window toward the snow-covered fields glowing under the full moon. A vibration in her chest rippled back to its source, somewhere out there. Before she saw the fresh tracks that led from the house to the opened barn door and from the barn door back to the house, she felt as if this were a story being retold without a teller. He wouldn't kill himself in the barn for another forty years, but what she didn't know, what she couldn't foresee, was already in motion. He was coming for her. She rushed to the door that led to the empty back room and turned the knob, even though she knew that the room on the other side of the door was the same as the room on this side. There was no inside and outside, not for her, not anymore.

Part 1

Character Witness

Several months after I came back from the therapy sessions at the Caron Foundation to my job in Tucson, I was sitting in my office trying not to fall asleep when the sixties-era phone on my desk started rattling. Because I had turned the volume all the way down, the ringer sounded like someone shaking a tambourine underwater. The phone was made from green plastic. The metal desk, the floor, and the bookcases were the same green. One dirty window high on the cinder-block wall framed a pigeon that stood looking in at me. This was where I worked, at a university.

When I picked up the receiver, a woman's voice said, "May I speak with Mr. Brown?" This didn't sound like a student. Students rarely called the office.

The woman on the phone said, "Is Susan Wende your mother?"

In a process I didn't understand, the institutions my mother owed money to had sold her debt to a guy who drove an eighties Olds with no muffler or hubcaps. He'd come to my house several times asking about her, and each time I'd said I didn't know whom he was talking about. It was possible that this guy had sold her debt (presumably at a steep discount) to the woman on the phone.

"I am calling from the Pima County Correctional Facility," the woman said. "Your mother gave your name as a contact person. She is being held in the facility and is scheduled for arraignment at 7:00 p.m."

"But she's a grandmother," I said and fixed my stare on the pigeon in my window. My sister, Liz, had a child. I didn't.

"She was picked up on a warrant sweep for a class two felony."

"What did she do?" I didn't really want to hear the answer.

"I'm afraid I do not have that information," the woman said and hung up.

According to felonyguide.com, a class two felony carried a sentence of between three and eight years. As far as I could tell, the next step up from a class two was second-degree murder.

There was a knock on my office door, and a head in the shape of the Bell telephone logo appeared behind the frosted glass. A student. The one from Nebraska. I held still and hoped she couldn't see the outline of my head, though of course she could. I could see the outline of her head, so she could see the outline of my head. Normally, I was happy to meet with students. One of the things I liked about myself was a need to prove to the world that I could be helpful and useful. Teaching fulfilled this need. Today was different, though. After a minute-long standoff, her heels tapped to the end of the hall where she opened the door that led to the west side of the building.

I scooted to the east-side door. The Modern Languages Building, designed to thwart protest occupations in response to the student uprisings of the sixties, had no front or central area. Every exit, even the main entrance, felt like a back door. I jumped on my bike, pedaled standing up all the way to my house on Seventeenth Street, and once there drank a glass of lemonade I didn't enjoy.

From my closet, I removed my only suit, the same one I'd worn to the interview for my current job. I shaved, bathed, and put on the suit and tie. I also pulled on my vintage wingtips, which I hastily cleaned with Windex and toilet paper.

✳

My mother, who'd been living an hour south of Tucson with her boyfriend, Daryl, worked for a home-care company that sent her around to the homes of retirees. According to what she later told me, the home-care company had called recently and left a message saying, "You took some stuff from one of the clients." Later a detective called and left a message: "Lady, we gotta talk." She declined to return the calls. One of the rings she'd scooped up turned out to be worth $38,000, though her friends at the Cashbox Pawnshop only had given her $5,000. A week after the home-care company and the detective called, she was picked up in an unmarked car, cuffed, and driven to the Pima County Correctional facility, where a woman checked her underwear for weapons and insisted she change into an orange jumpsuit.

They took her picture and typed in her information. Then, according to what my mother later told me, "You go into an area where they offer you horrible sandwiches. It's called the *Pit*." She heard her name on a loudspeaker, but she refused to move. There were cells on the other side of the area with people lying on the floor and banging on bars. A Mexican guy named Pancho sitting next to her said they'd picked him up out of the canal. He'd jumped in to get away. When Pancho asked my mother what she was in for, and she said class two, he whistled and said, "Big time." She introduced herself to her other immediate neighbors, Pedro, Bobby, and "some skinhead" and told them she was class two. "I was not the *worst* person on earth," she later told me. "I didn't *kill* anyone!" Then she added, "It does help to know that there are people who are worse off. It makes a person feel better."

A woman in a pantsuit carrying a file folder approached and looked my mother sternly in the face. "Susan Wende?" the woman asked. "Did you hear me?" she asked again. "You are Susan Wende?"

"I heard you the first time," my mother snapped. She'd been sitting there for over an hour. She was worn out, she told the pantsuit woman, and she was hungry. She requested a chicken sandwich. Not the garbage they had on offer in the Pit. Would someone bring her a chicken sandwich? In stressful situations, my mother tended to slur, so they might have thought she was drunk at first, but she had quit drinking several years before. Unlike me, she had never attended AA, never gone into the hospital. One day, she simply quit.

Instead of offering my mother a chicken sandwich, the pantsuit woman read off the charges: "Class two felony, trafficking in stolen goods over thirty thousand dollars." The guys around my mother— the ones making her feel better because she was not as bad off as they were—suddenly perked up.

"Over thirty K. Jesus, lady," Pedro said. "How the hell'd you do that?"

Ignoring my mother's new admirers, the pantsuit woman said, "When the judge asks if you understand the charges, you stand up and say, 'Yes.' Do you understand what I'm saying to you now?"

"I'm not an idiot," my mother said.

✳

A couple miles across town, car keys in hand, I stood in the middle of the living room and stared at the floor. On the mantle above the fireplace sat a picture of my "wife Amy" (my mother always air-quoted) in a silver frame. Amy now lived in another state where she attended graduate school—a temporary situation that was starting to look permanent.

I looked around at the varnished woodwork, the lime plaster, and varnished floors. There wasn't one inch of the house I hadn't poured my sweat into over the last few years. It was a small house, only 750 square feet, but it was a 1920 bungalow, a piece of Tucson history, and I had brought it back from the edge of total disintegration. I needed to convey to the legal system that I was a person whose mother would not be swallowed by the system. I expected to try to post bail, though with two grand in my account success seemed unlikely. I scanned the room for anything that might help me and lifted the book I'd been reading, *Democracy in America, Volume I*, by Alexis de Tocqueville, first published in 1835. In the early 1830s, de Tocqueville visited the United States to study the young democracy and try to determine, essentially, if it made any sense. Volume I contains an analysis of how the courts, cities, and local governments formed. With the book and one of my writing notebooks tucked into my leather satchel, I stalked out the door to my 1966 vw bug. I sputtered over to the Pima County Correctional Facility, a windowless concrete box that, from the outside, might've been mistaken for an armory, a junior high, or a slaughterhouse. I parked far away from the other cars because I still clung to the idea that someday I would restore the vw to its original condition. I didn't want careless people denting the thoroughly dented sheet metal.

Finding, on the far side of the building, a set of big glass doors, I entered with my head high and my chest thrust out. If people thought I was important, they might let my mother go. I gave my name to a woman sitting behind a counter with a tiny pencil-sharpened nose and blue eyeliner. She didn't even look up when she told me I had to wait on the other side of the room in one of the plastic chairs. I had no idea how I should be feeling or responding until I saw the other people in the plastic chairs, all of whom, ages six to sixty, sat with slumped shoulders and limp faces—the universal expression of those resigned to the current bureaucracy. I was sure some of them had spent time in this room before. None of them wore suits.

I sat, crossed my legs like someone preparing to read in the Bodleian Library, took out *Democracy in America, Volume I,* and read until I found this: "In no country in the world does the law hold so absolute a language as in America; and in no country is the right of applying it vested in so many hands. The administrative power in the United States presents nothing either centralized or hierarchical in its constitution; this accounts for its passing unperceived. The power exists, but its representative is nowhere to be seen."

The part of my brain that saw and read these words had been disconnected from the part of my brain that comprehended language. My name was called, and I followed another woman to a smaller room with no windows and blinding fluorescent lights. I parked myself in another plastic chair and, hoping to find evidence that I was nothing like my new companions, my eyes wandered over their faces: several women with their children, a few old men, a young woman, maybe a sister or a girlfriend of someone who had been arrested, all of them with the same washrag expressions as the group in the first room. I wondered why some of us were in this room, while others had been left in the first room. One tired-looking woman about my age patted the head of her small child.

The room contained two doors. The one through which I had entered and another door on the opposite side of the room. Somewhere beyond the second door sat my mother. I thought of the news reports I'd read in the last several years about Arizona prison violence (several inmates had died in a two-week standoff the previous year) and the methods of Sheriff Arpaio, "America's Toughest Sheriff," who forced inmates in Maricopa County to wear pink underwear while they stood for hours outside in the heat of the sun.

At this point, I didn't know why she was in trouble. According to the web, class two felonies included armed bank robbery, armed robbery in general, car theft (though grand theft auto didn't usually rise to the class two), or drug muling across the border from Nogales. My mother had been involved with the Samaritans, a humanitarian group that left water in the desert for people crossing illegally. Recently some members of the group had been arrested. Maybe this was about her humanitarian work, though that was too much to hope for.

The white door to the inner chamber of the building opened, and a tall woman with frizzy hair entered carrying a clipboard. She wanted me to stand. I stood. She wanted my name. I said my name. I had to sign. I had to empty my pockets into a bowl. She wanted the leather satchel on my shoulder. Unhappily, I gave up the satchel. She also wanted my notebook—"no writing inside," she said. I didn't understand. "No writing inside," she repeated. I only heard "no writing." She looked (rather skeptically, I thought) at my tie and suit jacket. I was dressed for the junior prom. "You can't take notes inside," she explained and held out her hand. I gave her my notebook. "I am going to need that book, too," she said and pointed.

"*Democracy in America*?" I heard a faint whine in my voice.

"No writing," the woman repeated, speaking very slowly.

"I'm not going to write in this book," I said, indicating the book. "This book has already been written."

"No reading," she said and shifted her weight and her impatience to the other side of her body. I hoped that our moment of mutual incomprehension might underscore the subtext of my current predicament: I didn't belong here, my mother didn't belong here. At the very least, I'd thought to throw my mother's captors off balance with my tie and my sham intellectual posturing, but everyone who worked here was ready for people to give them a hard time, twenty-four hours a day, seven days a week.

"What are you going to do with the book?" I asked. I wanted to explain that though several of my mother's siblings had spent time in jail, prison and other institutions, my mother was not like them, not really. She'd had a terrible childhood, but that wasn't a reason to toss her into the system. I wanted to say what I was sure she herself would've said: this was a mistake. Maybe—probably—it was her mistake, but it was still a *mistake*. Under the circumstances, her circumstances (she was my mother), didn't she deserve a pass? If my mother wasn't special, then neither was I.

"I will need that pen, too," the woman said. I gave her the pen. "I will put them in a locker, and you can get them when you leave." The woman carried everything to a row of gray metal lockers. She opened one of the square doors and pushed the bag, the notebook, and the book inside.

"It doesn't lock?" I said, and she scowled at me.

"No one is going to take it," she said.

This didn't seem obvious to me. I supposed I should assume that the only criminals in the building had been restrained. I didn't assume that at all. *Free the criminals and lock up the captors!* I wanted to yell but didn't because it was exactly the kind of thing my mother said to people all the time.

Now I felt naked. My hands darted up and down my thighs like nervous sheepdogs. I had nothing but my garden party tie to separate me from the others in the room. The woman who'd taken my book and notebook told us all to stand. We were herded past the lockers, down a long hallway, and into a large white room with no windows and only one door. All the other rooms had featured two doors—the one you entered from the familiar world and the one that led deeper into the building. Overhead fluorescent lights buzzed like insects. Two flat screens suspended from the ceiling. The screen on the left showed an empty desk in a small gray room. The screen on the right showed a row of empty plastic chairs. On the right-hand screen, several orange jumpsuits shuffled in front of the row of chairs. Hispanic men in their twenties and thirties, one older black man, one wiry white boy, and finally, at the end of the row, my mother, half the size of her smallest companion. They all shared similar expressions.

The pantsuit woman who'd taken my book stood below the screens and offered the following prologue: Our "families" were in the detention center on the right-hand screen. "In a few moments the judge will appear on the left-hand screen," she said. The judge could see the accused people on his own screen, and the accused people could see the judge on a screen in the detention center. Neither group could see us. We were outside the loop.

When I saw my mother's hands shaking, I stood up, walked to the front of the room, and demanded to see her. "She is a grandmother," I said. "This is ridiculous."

"You can't," the woman said. "Sit down."

I would not sit down.

"Can I get a message to her and let her know I am here?" I asked.

"Sit down or you will have to leave," the woman said.

I sat down.

Overweight and cranky and wearing bright white basketball shoes, the judge arrived on screen and perched behind his desk. He glanced impatiently to his left, apparently in the direction of the TV screen that displayed the accused. A voice off-screen called names. A woman appeared and tapped one of the men in orange on the shoulder. The man stood and the judge read off the charges: assault, battery, robbery. Another off-screen voice asked in Spanish if the man understood the charges. "Sí," the man said, and, after the woman tapped him on the shoulder again, he sat down and looked at his feet. It wasn't clear to me that he understood anything at all. Finally, the judge said my mother's name, Susan Wende. My mother stood and squinted at the screen that must have shown the judge. Then she squinted at the camera, at me. She wasn't wearing her glasses.

"Susan Wende," the judge said, and she nodded. He then read off the charges: class two felony, trafficking in stolen goods over thirty thousand dollars. Unfortunately, the judge looked a bit like my mother's father.

"Now wait a minute," my mother said, raising her index finger into the air. "I only got five thousand for that stuff. I mean it doesn't seem fair you're saying it was—what?—thirty-some thousand when I never saw that money!" The judge did not look happy.

"Susan Wende," the judge said, "do you understand the charges?" She didn't, not at all. She turned and waved at me. I waved back, even though I knew she couldn't see me. She couldn't know that I was even there.

"Susan Wende," the judge said again, louder this time.

"Yes!" she said, rolling her eyes, clearly irritated. "That's me!"

"Do you understand the charges?"

She wanted to tell him to fuck off, I knew she did, and I tried to warn her not to by waving my hands and shaking my head. The woman who'd stolen my books ordered me to stop, but I didn't. I kept waving. My mother faced the judge and opened her mouth to answer.

"No," I whispered. "Don't do it."

"All right, yes, I understand the charges," she said, and she sat down in defeat. I was relieved—but also disappointed.

＊

Reunited with my leather satchel, I returned to the front desk of the building where I felt shocked to be free. The woman behind the desk told me my mother would be released on her own recognizance (OR), also known as personal recognizance (PO), a kind of no-cost bail. Apparently, as a first-time offender and elderly person, they didn't consider her a flight risk. But she was not a first-time offender. She was first-time at getting caught, which is different. And in my opinion, she certainly *was* a flight risk. I was confident I would have to talk her out of trying to drive her unregistered car down to Mexico.

I didn't share any of these thoughts with the woman behind the desk, who told me that as soon as the officers "processed" her, my mother would be set free, pending trial, and I could take her home. Deciding to wait in the parking lot, I moved the VW to a spot in front of the gray door where the woman at the front desk had said my mother would soon appear. An hour passed without the door opening, so I returned to the front desk where the same woman pretended she'd never seen me before.

"You told me she'd be released," I said.

"I'm sorry," she said. "What are you asking me?" I explained, she called someone in the bowels of the facility, nodded a few times, read my mother's name off a sticky note, nodded a few more times.

"Your mother should've been released," the woman said.

"*Should have been*?" I said. "What does that mean?"

"Yes," the woman replied. "She should've been released a half hour ago."

I took a deep breath and stared at the enormous air ducts bolted to the concrete ceiling. Cool air washed over my hot cheeks and teased the bleached bangs of the woman staring up at me. So my mother had slipped loose from reality and now swam free somewhere in the past conditional tense.

"Do you know what time, exactly, she 'should have' been released?"

"Should've been a half hour ago. Like I said." The woman, Linda, still smiled but clearly wanted me to move on.

As I turned onto Seventeenth Street, I saw from a block away that someone had switched on all the lights of my house. My mother lived with Daryl an hour south, but she didn't have her car. I assumed she'd taken a cab to my house and used the spare key I'd given her. When I parked outside the gate, I could see, along the roofline, piles of roof shingles stacked by Daryl, and I was reminded that my mother had recently convinced me to hire him to redo my roof.

The day before Daryl and I had stood next to the house and tried to hash out our disagreement about the job. He'd crossed his arms over his chest. He had a habit of standing very close and at a *slight* angle so that he seemed to be having a conversation with someone standing next to me. Between phrases that seemed meant for me, he grumbled either to himself or to an apparition standing nearby. He was fit for sixty-five, kept his hair closely cropped, and never smiled.

Always furrowed his brow. At first, the previous month, he'd agreed to one price but then later changed his mind and wanted 25 percent more so he could hire a helper. He had originally said he easily could do the job without a helper. Now he was saying the job couldn't be done without a helper. If I paid him 25 percent more, I would be paying him the same amount I would pay a roofer, which I couldn't afford.

In 1967 Daryl fell on his head during army basic training. Dizzy and disoriented, he went AWOL rather than consult with doctors. Consequently, he spent a year in the brig before they discovered that he had a traumatic brain injury and gave him a medical discharge for his woes. Since then, he'd traveled the country in a converted Airstream trailer and practiced astrology and bio-touch therapy. Daryl had many skills: he could predict the fate of a relationship based on the birth dates of the participants; he had converted (for reasons connected to the end of capitalism) his truck to run on propane; he'd worked, I'd been told, as a Feng Shui consultant, house painter, and bicycle mechanic. The one thing he was not was a roofer. I hoped I wouldn't find him inside, where his presence would remind me that I never should've listened to my mother about hiring him.

My mother lay on the sofa with her feet up and her arm draped over her forehead. When I asked her how she'd gotten here, she shooed me away with her fingers.

"Pedro and I shared a cab," she said.

"Who the hell is Pedro?"

"Pedro's another criminal. Now can you be quiet? I've had a day. And don't be upset because I don't want to hear it. I was the only felon they let go home. Except Pedro, who is no threat to anyone, I can tell you that."

I went into my bedroom and took my notebook out of my leather satchel.

"What're you doing in there?" my mother asked. It was a tiny house; she wasn't that far away.

"Nothing," I said. I was writing down everything the woman from the jail had told me not to write down.

"This whole thing should go in our book," my mother said, "don't you think? The people will love this."

I'd talked to her about writing down some of the stories from her life and my own life. She called it "our book" and hoped it would make a lot of money, even though I'd told her it wouldn't. Even if I showed it to her, as I would, and sought her approval before putting anything out in the world, as I would, it still would be written from my life.

In part because the border between us—where she ends and I begin—has always been uncertain, I want those involved in this true tale to succeed, and as a result, maybe I to some extent have turned my mother into a character to salvage her for my own sake. Maybe it's impossible to stand outside myself to see who I am, to see who she is. I don't know. I do know that if I fail to see and treat her as fully human, I will fail both of us.

*

Greg Berger, a public defender in a threadbare sports coat, was trying to figure out how to bust down the charges to something lighter but confessed that the "evidence was not good." He added, "Arizona is really tough. Your mother took the jewelry and didn't try to give it back. She did the opposite."

I pointed out that she had no criminal history. She had stolen from me and owed money to many of the institutions who had agreed to do business with her, but those things didn't count.

I called my father in Maine and told him what had happened. His response was silence followed by a long sigh. They'd been divorced for over fifteen years at this point. After I went on for some time about the details, he finally said, "*That* family," meaning my mother's family. "There's something wrong with them. All of them."

I was part of "that family" as well, at least genetically, but I didn't point this out.

He realized his mistake and said, "At least you didn't grow up in *that* house. At least you're not related to him."

He meant my mother's stepfather, the Nazi. I was related to her actual father, the violent, abusive alcoholic. Six of one.

I asked him if he thought I should hire a private lawyer.

"With what money?" he said. "That will cost a fortune. Class two? I assume your mother has no money."

"Except for what she got for the, you know, stolen jewelry."

"Yeah," he said. "I think you'd better count on the public defender." I had hoped, against all reason, that my father would have a grand, sweeping, and preferably immediate solution. Maybe he'd offer up thousands of dollars, which, aside from his modest retirement account, he didn't have (he'd been a civil servant for most of my childhood), or maybe he'd take on the case himself. He wasn't a criminal lawyer, nor was he licensed to practice in Arizona.

I told him I'd talked to Greg Berger, my mother's public defender, and he'd mentioned that character witness letters might help. Greg called me an "upstanding member of the community." A perfect character witness.

"Sure," my father mumbled. He had a sixth sense for "the ask."

"And you," I said, "because you were in the Maine attorney general's office."

He groaned, grumbled for thirty seconds, and was silent. My father's last interaction with my mother involved her suing him for assault and abuse, an accusation that turned out to be false. I had never seen my father act violently toward me or anyone else. She'd also accused me of abuse and threatened to sue me multiple times. As far as I could tell, among the men she'd known well, the only ones she had not sued or threatened to sue were the ones who actually had abused her: her father and stepfather.

At least from the outside, we had at one time resembled a conventional New England family in our colonial house in Hallowell, Maine. We hadn't been rich, we hadn't been poor. Our income straddled the border between middle and lower middle class, and we lived solely on my father's government salary. Maine, in those days, was poorer than it is now. My father had his job and my grandparents had Social Security and a pension with enough savings to buy a used car whenever their current car rusted out from under them. Despite the obvious reality of our financial circumstances, my father's parents and the rest of the family would have shuddered at the idea that we were lower middle or even middle class—we were fallen from some greater height that superseded the concept of class. My grandfather was the architect of this mythology that we were better than other people precisely because we didn't make money. All I knew was that we could only drink one glass of milk each a day and that instead of a sofa in the room where we had the black and white TV we had a bare dirty mattress on a metal frame. I was happy to tell kids what my father did for a living, but I didn't want them coming over to the house to see the peeling dirty yellow linoleum or the piles of empty wine bottles and cigarette butts and the soot-covered walls.

Though our house was built of bricks and our cars made by the General Motors Company—and though my father's job was serious and, in ways I didn't quite understand, *important*—we struggled to maintain the illusion that we were not one of "those" people who lived in falling down houses by the river, whose kids went to school in T-shirts in the winter.

My father's family was from Maine, New Hampshire, and Massachusetts and had some history in the town, where a great uncle had lived when he was governor of the state in 1856. My father's ancestors had been established New Englanders—farmers, colonial ship captains—and they'd come over early on the *Mayflower* and in the subsequent waves of pilgrim migration. My mother, born into a family who had come to America as poor German immigrants, was from a small town outside Buffalo, New York, and had met my father when she was visiting Maine. They dated off and on until they finally married. After a while they seemed to forget whatever had originally drawn them together, probably because they were first drawn together when they were teenagers.

When I was young, I knew something was off with us and particularly with me—I just didn't know what. We didn't seem to be missing anything. Most kids I knew had fathers who were absent to some extent—they went to work all day, sometimes on the weekends, too, and left the house to the mothers. Even when my parents sat in the same room together, they were miles apart. That vast empty space was where my sister and I lived. We were separated by six years—a lifetime. My mother was the only one who passed through my orbit for any length of time.

Divorce had served its purpose for my parents—they both went their separate ways. For my mother and I, it was not so easy because we couldn't—or felt we couldn't—go our separate ways. What developed between my mother and me cannot be isolated to a single incident, a misstep or transgression of language or the body that can be unbraided from the rest of my life. Her actions were my actions, her hands on my body were my transgressions, her way of seeing me was my way of seeing, her words my words. She was my life, the air I breathed; there was no way of standing outside my life in order to determine whether what was happening was abnormal or not. To the outside world, to the rest of the family, even to my father, it may have looked normal enough, but my mother and I had our own secret reality that no one could see into, and I could not see out of.

"What am I supposed to say?" my father said over the phone, more to himself than to me, it seemed.

In fact, I had an answer to this question because I'd already asked the public defender what he should say.

"Well, what a great mother she was and a solid citizen."

"A solid citizen?"

"Back when you knew her? Maybe solid is too much. Maybe just an okay citizen?"

"I don't know," he said. "A letter, with my name on it?"

We'd never talked in detail about my mother in any kind of honest or straightforward way. She'd asked him for a divorce shortly after we moved from Hallowell an hour south to Portland. I knew that much. He'd wanted to work things out; she hadn't. Did he feel she was getting what she deserved on some level? Did he think that she cared about people in the way a good citizen should—selflessly, altruistically? I doubted it. She'd been absent and spent some time under psychiatric care when I was young. No diagnosis was ever mentioned to me.

"Has she been seeing anyone? A doctor, I mean?" my father asked.

I said that I didn't think she was. I'd suggested she see a shrink many times. The last time I'd suggested it, she'd said, "You would *love* that, wouldn't you? Get me locked away forever." By way of reply, I might've said, "Yes, that *would* be great." My mother and I both tended to forget the worst things we'd said to each other over the years.

"Here's what I'll do," my father said. "You write the letter, and I'll sign it. How about that?"

I said yes because I needed whatever help I could get, but now I had to write my letter and his letter—son and former husband.

I spent several days worrying about how to address the letters. "Your Honor" sounded old fashioned or like something from a TV show. "To Whom It May Concern" sounded like a recommendation letter. "Dear Jurors." It wasn't a jury trial—yet. "Members of the Court." I had no idea what that even meant. I could have asked the public defender or my father what to say, but I couldn't bear to speak to anyone about the letters. In the end, I went with "Your Honor."

Your Honor:
My name is Jason Brown, and I am writing on behalf of my mother, Susan Wende. I live in Tucson and am an associate professor of English at the University of Arizona. [All true.]
    As long as I have lived in Arizona, my mother and I have seen each other on a weekly basis. [Not true, not at all. I avoided my mother whenever possible and sometimes went months without seeing her even though she lived only a short distance away.] When I was young growing up in Maine, my mother worked for many years as a special education teacher. [This was sort of true—she worked part-time for a shorter

period. She may have been fired.] She was a devoted and compassionate teacher; she showed amazing resilience in one of the hardest jobs I can imagine. [This may have been true—I had no idea. I never visited her work. When she talked about work, or about anything really, I often entered a fugue-like dissociative state aided by alcohol until I was forced to stop drinking at age twenty-one. I thought it unwise at this point to mention in the letter my years of sobriety, preceded by years of blackouts, car crashes, job losses, etc. I had been a binge drinker, my mother a maintenance drinker, but this distinction didn't seem relevant to the task at hand.] After my parents' divorce in 1989, my mother has sustained one personal and financial setback after another. [One hundred percent true. Possibly setbacks of her own making, but setbacks nonetheless.] Because of her grave and damaging mistake, she can now no longer work as a caregiver, and she faces financial destitution. [All true.] I know she regrets her mistake [This was not necessarily true—I was pretty sure she thought the old woman she had stolen from deserved to share her wealth a little] both because it was so harmful to the woman she worked for, and because it was self-destructive. [Doubtful—I was fairly sure she thought the only self-destructive aspect of this event was getting caught.] She is eager, I know, to overcome her difficulties and to make reparations. [Zero percent true.] She is a good person and has been a caring mother and grandmother. [Well, she had threatened to sue me, given me gallons of booze before I was thirteen, behaved toward me in a way that several doctors had described as incest, hit on my best friend in high school, and destroyed our family's finances.]

The second letter was shorter but much harder to write.

Your Honor:
My name is Rufus Brown, and I am an attorney at Brown and Burke in Portland, Maine. I have worked in private practice

in Portland since 1985. Before that I was a Deputy Attorney General for the State of Maine.

Susan Wende and I were married for twenty-two years, until 1989. While we were married, she was a good mother to our children and a devoted teacher in the public school system. I know that she has faced many personal and financial struggles in recent years, and I can only imagine that her recent transgressions were acts of desperation for which she is suffering regret and shame. She is a good person who cares about people and loves her family. I know she will move beyond this event, make reparations, and strive to be a productive member of her family and the community.

My sole purpose in these letters was to sound like someone other than myself—a detached and loving son/former husband who saw the world through an objective lens. *Family, community, reparations, productive, regret*—all words a lawyer would apply to a good citizen. Not, unfortunately, words anyone who knew my mother would associate with her.

The public defender suggested that my mother write her own letter, essentially serving as a character witness for herself.

Your Honor:
I am very remorseful concerning my involvement in this case in which I took advantage of and victimized an elderly, defenseless person. I have never before been involved in criminal behavior, and this has reflected very negatively on my character, hurting both me and my family.

Losing my caregiving job this past June was a direct consequence of my behavior. My work experience is in the area of social services and teaching. Now, however, I cannot work in either of these fields.

I have had difficulty economically, an uneven work history, and have failed to establish community. I think that probation will give me the support I need to build community and economic stability.

Thank you for your consideration in this matter.

I didn't write this letter—neither did my mother. This letter was written mostly by Greg. My mother would have talked about class war, the 1 percent, the migrant deaths on the border, and the nefarious permutations of the empire. She was a diehard proponent of speaking her mind. I would've preferred a letter written by her, but I was grateful, under the circumstances, that we were both taking a more practical course of action.

＊

I showed up for the hearing at the Pima County Courthouse, in a small courtroom that smelled of dust and old socks. I'd been told by my mother that Greg had arranged a plea agreement: a guilty plea in exchange for busting it down to class three. Apparently, though, there was no guarantee from the court that she would get off with probation. She might plead guilty and still have to serve time. She sat in a wooden chair next to Greg and looked at her hands on the table. I sat as far away as possible while still being in the same room. Daryl, sitting in the other corner, waved to me several times while I pretended not to notice. I didn't want to be on Daryl's team. I wanted him to finish replacing my roof so I could forget that I'd been foolish enough to hire him in the first place.

"Do you feel taking this plea agreement is in your best interest?" the judge asked my mother. "If you are sentenced to prison, you would have to serve at least 85 percent of the sentence in prison before you would be eligible for release. Then you would have to serve 15 percent of the sentence outside of prison under a community supervision program. Do you understand those possibilities?"

"Yes," she said in a subdued tone. She was following the script, which was unusual. Her eyes were wide, her back hunched.

The judge explained that the maximum fine for any felony was $150,000 plus restitution for economic loss to the victim. No one could promise her exactly what the sentence would be. It would depend on the "facts of the case and on you and your background and any criminal history that you might have. Do you understand?"

My mother nodded slowly, but the judge said she had to speak out loud, for the record, so she said, "Yes." I could tell from the way she grimaced that this was painful for her. Above all else, she'd once told me, she hated when men told her what to do.

The judge catalogued my mother's crimes. My mother had to say yes to every detail. She had taken the rings—that wasn't in dispute—but according to her testimony, she'd truly thought that the rings were being given to her. I could tell the judge had decided that no one would believe that a stranger would give away a $38,000 ring for no reason.

At the end of the proceedings, Greg delivered a dispassionate pitch for leniency based on my mother's "age and the fact she's never had any contact with the justice system." Also, because she was "at a point in her life when things were going very poorly for her financially and emotionally."

Halfway through Greg's speech, I had lowered my forehead against the back of the chair in front me and squeezed my eyes shut. I was also at a point in my life where, as Greg had said of my mother, "things were going very poorly." I was married to a woman who lived in another state. We didn't even like each other, but for some reason we couldn't pull apart. I had very few friends, just people I talked to at work. I had little interest in my job, little interest in reading or writing. Tucson—all of Arizona, for that matter—felt like a color-enhanced diorama; I was a clay figure with a painted hat.

The judge spoke of my mother's clean record and the excellent character witness testimonies. Finally, he concluded: "I will place you on probation for a period of five years to begin as of today's date." My mother nodded her head slightly. I thought she might raise a fist or cry, but she sat perfectly still like a chipmunk hoping to escape the notice of a cat.

"I'm anticipating that you'll get a job in the near future." The judge's eyes widened in anticipation of her answer.

My mother shrugged. She knew that she had to actually speak for the record. "Sure," she said.

*

Several days after my mother's hearing, I turned off Fourth Avenue onto Seventeenth Street at the end of the day and noticed activity on the roof of my house. Daryl getting down to business. Work had stopped during the "legal troubles"—Daryl's idea, not mine. He needed to support my mother, he'd said. When I stepped out of the car, I looked up and saw a second person standing on the peak of the roof. Not as tall as Daryl, wearing a yellow blouse and knee socks and with one end of a rope tied around her waist and the other around the chimney: my mother with a load of asphalt shingles in her arms. Daryl's hammer rose and pounded on a nail. When she noticed me walking up to the house, my mother smiled and tried unsuccessfully to free one of her hands to wave. Her mouth moved and Daryl's head popped up. I'd refused to hire him a helper, so he'd tied my mother to the roof. He watched me for a moment before he dipped below the roofline and resumed swinging.

"You have to get down from there," I called to my mother. As long as she teetered on the edge, so did I. Her missteps always had been and always would feel like my own. I rushed forward ready to catch her if she fell. She peered over the lip of the roof with her chin tucked in.

"Come down," I said sternly, as if speaking to a child.

"Can't you see," she said, raising her eyebrows and nodding, "that I have a job to do?"

She seemed genuinely disappointed that I didn't understand— that I never would understand—and with her arms full of shingles, she turned and climbed back to the top of the house.

The Guest

I considered my mother remarkably fortunate, especially in tough-on-crime Arizona, to get away with probation. In the months after her appearance before the judge, she started driving north from Green Valley to Tucson to see her probation officer. Whenever she could catch me at home, she wanted to talk about "the situation," which at first I took to mean her felony. But no. Apparently, she and Daryl were having trouble, and she wanted to know when I would stop trying to control his mind.

"You don't want the two of us to be together," she told me one hot day while we stood next to the lemon tree I'd planted. I was feeding the tree water through a slow-drip hose. I had devoted a disproportionate amount of energy to cultivating the tree. Much like me, it was not meant to survive in this climate, and particularly where I'd planted it, in a slab of caliche soil as solid as airport tarmac. I had used an electric jackhammer to excavate a four-foot-deep, four-foot-wide hole, inserted a PVC pipe to feed water to the bottom, and bedded the tree in organic planting soil. On cold nights in the winter, I lay a little tree blanket over the branches. The tree and I were conducting an experiment in desert survival; the browning leaves did not bode well for either one of us.

"You're destroying my relationship," my mother said as I picked at the leaves.

"You can go out with whomever you want to," I said in a calm voice I'd rehearsed. "But Daryl did a terrible job on my roof. I don't want to speak to him."

"He worked very hard on that roof."

"I didn't pay him to work hard; I paid him to fix it."

My attitude, my mother explained, was the problem here. My attitude was not conducive to her happiness. She didn't see why she shouldn't be happy, just like everyone else.

I said I wasn't so sure "everyone else" was all that happy.

She nodded, seeming to take this point into consideration.

Two weeks after meeting with my mother next to my lemon tree to discuss her boyfriend, I heard someone shouting my name from outside my front gate. I was in the kitchen, trying to summon the energy to boil a pot of pasta. I always locked the gate, in theory against criminals, but really because of my mother. At one time I'd let her have a spare key, but recently too many things had gone missing in the house, so I had taken it back.

Outside, my mother stood on the other side of the gate pointing at the lock. I could tell she'd been crying and worried that something had happened with the police or her parole officer. I looked over her shoulder at her car full of trash bags, a lamp, and what looked like a suitcase. Also, there was a cat in the front seat. Attila the Hun II. The passenger seat was leaned all the way back and covered with a sleeping bag and a pillow.

"Have you been sleeping in the car?" I already knew the answer to this question. The real question was how long had she been sleeping in her car? I didn't really want to know.

"I know how *busy* you are. But I need a place to stay," she said. "Daryl took off in his Airstream."

"How long ago?"

"A while."

I wanted a bit more clarification before unlocking the gate. After my mother had first moved to Arizona, she had lived with an older guy who had died and left her without a cent. Since then, she had pieced together temporary jobs and places to live, but she had always been on the verge of having no money and nowhere to live. She had convinced her lawyer Greg Berger and ultimately the court that she'd had some bad luck financially and had suffered from a temporary lapse of judgment that would be corrected once she got back on her feet. In my lifetime, though, she'd never been able to sustain full-time employment for long. Ever since she had left my father and exhausted the alimony he owed her, she had been in danger of becoming permanently homeless.

While I wondered if I couldn't just say *no, you can't come in,* another part of me felt exhilarated by the idea of crashing headlong into the tangled chaos of her life. My mother was one of the few people in my life I felt an actual connection to.

I knew that I couldn't reach out and help her up without tumbling forward myself, but I told myself I had no choice. I had to help her because she was my mother, and because the men in her life had always failed her, particularly her father and stepfather. My father had been remote to her, it seemed. I'd always felt I had to compensate for these men, no matter the cost to myself, and even as the effort to do so pushed me toward becoming the kind of man I had promised myself I would never be. Angry, self-pitying, trapped.

I carried her things into the house, piled them in the front room, and asked her how long she thought she would be visiting. She sat on my sofa and sighed.

"I'm not visiting," she said.

＊

The last time I'd lived with my mother was the year I'd dropped out of college at twenty after authorities briefly wanted to admit me to a psyche ward for saying I didn't want to live anymore. I'd slipped out of the building before they could lock me up and felt proud of myself before figuring out that no one cared. At the college, I'd had trouble with drinking and been forced to meet with their doctors and the Dean of Students several times about black outs and public disturbances. One night I threw most of my furniture out of the window of my upper-story dorm room. My mattress, desk chair, bookshelf and whatnot crashed into the pavement of the parking lot without killing anyone. Their medical advice was that I stop drinking.

I asked my mother if I could stay with her in her fourth-floor attic apartment overlooking the Fore River in Portland, Maine. I had no money, nowhere else to go. I thought of this as a temporary arrangement, but after six months I was still there. Freighters and oil tankers passed up and down the river at all times of the day and night—a reminder of the practical activities of the world that had nothing to do with me. My parents had been divorced for several years by now, and my mother was living on temporary alimony from my father, which was scheduled to run out in less than a year. Her plan was to get a teaching job in a war zone. People in war zones still needed to go to school, she informed me, and were not fussy about teacher accreditation. She had a lead in a hot spot in Chiapas.

Our geriatric dog, Blondie, had trouble walking up the stairs (she had heart disease, she had liquid in her lungs, she had arthritis, she was mostly blind, she was mostly deaf), so I had to carry her outside each time she had to go. My mother's cat, Attila the Hun I, sat on the sofa or the windowsill and watched me from under drooping eyelids. I worked for a place in downtown Portland called the Cookie Mama, where I baked and sold oversized cookies to tourists, lunching lawyers, and other people I detested. Mostly I got stoned and ate cookies all day while writing poems in my head to the saleswoman at a pottery store two doors down.

One night when I started to hear scraping sounds from inside the walls of the apartment, I came out of the bedroom the size of a closet where I slept and stood in the dark of the main room. My mother opened her door to her room and looked through the picture window toward the Fore River. The noises were not just in the walls of my bedroom. My mother walked up to the wall and leaned close to the plaster.

There'd been some hope before speaking with my mother about the noises in the walls that there was nothing in the walls at all except squirrels or mice. Maybe branches scraped the roof. Maybe the sound came from Marginal Way, the street below the row of Victorians that fronted the wharves on the Fore River. Now I noticed that the wall plaster flaked off as it had in our house in Hallowell, and there was always more to take its place, as if it continued to grow. In some places, though, the lath showed through like ribs. Not squirrels, not rodents. I was convinced that the apartment itself was alive. My mother, who stared at the wall for hours, seemed to share my conviction.

I was drinking at this time but not with anyone. There was no one else I could talk to about what was happening. There was no one out there except my mother. Even people I knew, the other members of my family, my high school friends like Dan or Rick, seemed like people I'd never seen before. They knew my name, I knew where they lived, but I couldn't reach them. I felt as if I were standing waist-deep in water at the bottom of a well. People passed back and forth in front of the tiny circle of light far above, but no one paused to look down.

One day I came home after losing my job at the Cookie Mama (they said I was giving away the cookies for free, and this was true, I was giving away the cookies for free) and found masking tape on all the windows facing the driveway and the other apartment buildings. My mother sat on the linoleum in the kitchen. When I asked her about the masking tape, she said there were cracks in all the windows and the cold air was getting inside.

There were no cracks, and the tape seemed arranged in a pattern of symbols, though not symbols that I recognized—half-formed stars, broken squares, blobs. She said all right, all right—it was a message to the neighbor.

"Which neighbor?" I demanded, but she shook her head.

"*Which* neighbor?"

Her face turned rabid, and she flew at me as she swept cat food cans, salt and pepper shakers, wine bottles, everything sitting between us, onto the floor.

Twenty minutes later the man who lived in the bottom half of a duplex across the street pulled into his driveway and got out with his young son. My mother crouched on the floor behind the sofa and covered her head as if someone was about to hit her.

"When he knocks on the door, tell him . . . I'm not here!" she said. I watched as the man unloaded his groceries and followed his son inside without looking in our direction at all.

She went into the bathroom and came back with a pair of scissors. Clamping a bunch of hair at the back of her head, she started to chop it off. Finally, her face relaxed.

"There, maybe now the walls will shut up," she said, and I thought she might be right. Maybe the walls would shut up. Her hair, from what I could see, was all different lengths, standing out in odd directions, almost bare in certain spots. She patted it down with her palm, stared out the window, and told me about her dance classes, and how she'd met so many interesting people there, though they were *so* into their bodies. Her voice sounded different, too young. I had an eerie sense that she was possessed by her thirteen-year-old self.

She had rolled her eyes over the word *bodies*, and I began to feel paralyzed. Maybe, she said, she would become a dancer. Though she was close to fifty, her friend Mora (who'd also divorced her husband and started over) had told her this was a turning point, a new beginning: anything was possible now that she was free of the marriage. She might sell things, she might work in a little store for a while, where pleasant people came into the shop—there was plenty of time for it all—but in the end she would return to *the children*. It was true—animals and children seemed to like her. She sat on the floor and covered her face with her hands. "I have to do this," she said as our dog Blondie came over to lick her face.

"Do what?"

I thought I half understood what she was telling me. There was a force inside of her driving her to tear everything down, starting with her marriage and now herself. I recognized a similar force inside of me. Some kind of mental illness, it was hard to deny that now. The phrase *mental illness* flashed in my head like a roadside construction sign. I felt rather than understood that this force was also some form of infantile rebellion. The lives we'd been given, the lives we'd constructed, were no longer tolerable.

The doctor at the clinic who wrote me scripts for anxiety pills told me I needed to see a psychiatrist. I hadn't even told him about the noises in the walls, that I thought the walls had started to smell like cooked broccoli, and that I harbored an untrue but persistent belief that the apartment itself was a living thing. I hadn't told anyone about this and had no intention of doing so in the future. The last thing I needed was someone informing me that I was "nuts." At least the doctor hadn't suggested I go to AA. I was careful not to smell of booze or pot when I saw him, but when I abstained my eye started to twitch uncontrollably. I asked him if he really thought a shrink was necessary. He was a skinny man with a trimmed beard who always looked tired. He was probably tired of me.

"Yeah," he said and nodded, "you need to see someone."

I must've seemed doubtful, which I was. I told him I'd just lost my job selling cookies and didn't have any insurance or money. He asked me if I might try my father. I forgot I'd told him my father was a lawyer in town. Weeks passed when I forgot that my father even lived in town, just two miles away.

"Don't you think your father would want to help you?"

This was an interesting question. My mother was also of the opinion that my father should "do something to help," though she thought he should start by helping her. Specifically, by giving her more money. Even though she'd been the one to leave him, he *owed* her, and, according to her, he was rich! Until a few years ago, when we'd left Hallowell for Portland, he'd worked for the state earning about as much as a Maine teacher. Like most Americans, the only thing he owned was debt. My mother was his ex-wife, I was an adult—he *owed* us nothing except a few more months of alimony—yet my mother's sense of entitlement was a drug I seemed to ingest without questioning. He didn't so much owe us because he was her ex-husband and my father, but because he was one of *them*, able of mind and body. To my mother, the world broke down into two groups—those who should be helped and those who should carry the rest of us around. A seductively simple idea. At the same time, though, she refused to consider the idea that there might be anything "wrong" with her.

My father subscribed to the mythology that a person must bend fate to their own will, while my mother believed a person bent and eventually broke under the tyranny of other people's wills. In the Manichean cosmology of our family, my mother thought my father had oppressed her, while my father thought my mother lived in a fantasy. He and I had never discussed whether her fantasies might be a sign of illness. He hadn't offered any thoughts on the matter, except to suggest that she lacked character. I knew that I lacked character.

I showed up at my father's work, a large law firm in a four-story converted warehouse in the middle of the city's commercial district. Though I didn't have a specific agenda, I was emboldened by my doctor's comment that surely my father would want to do something even though he was remarried and had my younger sister to raise.

The bottom floor housed a title company the firm owned, and the lobby featured a large plaque with the names of all the members of the firm, including my father's name in brass lettering set against the grain of the wooden panel. That I would never be able to close the gap between where he was on that wall and where I stood in my dirty jeans and canvas coat had to be his fault, but I didn't know how exactly. I had no perspective. I'd spent most of my life on the coast of Maine, where there were few signs of conspicuous wealth outside of summer enclaves and few signs of extreme poverty. My father's family (my father, a lawyer, his father, a teacher, and his father's father who owned a barrel factory in Lewiston) included a history of men who'd forged their own way in life. I was failing to join their world because there was something wrong with me.

The doors opened on a wood-paneled reception with coffee tables and Persian carpets. It occurred to me that I probably smelled of pot and booze in addition to sweat. For some reason, I hadn't cleaned up for this. I tried to reverse back into the elevator, but the doors had already closed. I said my father's first and last name to the receptionist and sat down on a leather sofa in front of a *National Geographic*. A few minutes later the woman led me down a hallway to the far side of the building. She knocked on a heavy, varnished door, and I heard his voice saying we should come in. He sat behind a large mahogany desk in the corner of his office. One set of windows behind him faced the harbor, another set looked down Fore Street toward the Fore River. My mother lived a mile or so in that direction. So did I.

He dismissed the receptionist and pointed to a chair across from his desk. He'd worked here since he'd left his position with the state. If not rich, he was certainly powerful, at least from my perspective. To me the law was about rationality and authority in the social structure. He had it. I didn't. It might've occurred to me that in relative terms, in historical terms, my father and I occupied similar territory in the social structure. It didn't occur to me at least in part because I suffered from the myopia of psychic pain. The person who drops an anvil on their toe can think of little else but their toe. No one is more possessed by greed than a severely depressed person. Other people are no longer real. They are potential tormentors or potential saviors, and encounters with others only serve to remind the depressed person that no one can really help them.

It wasn't that my father had not reached out to me—he had reached out when he and my mother were getting divorced, and he had called me when I dropped out of college. I had been hostile and unfriendly and assumed that he knew what was going on with me even though there was no way he could know. Sitting in his office, I felt rejected. It never occurred to me that he might feel the same way. Trapped in myself, I had no way of asking him what it might feel like to have a teenage son glare at you year after year.

We had yet to say a word to each other, but it felt as if we'd come to the same judgment. I had made up our minds that we were strangers to one another. He didn't want me to ask him for help. In seeing my debilitating need and my failure to achieve independence as a cancer on my spirit that could only be starved out of me, I imagined that he'd aligned himself with the myth of the self-reliant hero who battles his own darker nature to become monolithically himself. My grandfather landing at D-Day, his brother flying cover above in his Thunderbolt. An uncle in the First Calvary in the Ia Drang. All of these men had managed to fulfill the roles society had prepared for them. I'd just gotten fired from the Cookie Mama.

I couldn't help but side with what I thought my father must be thinking. I'd been given more of a chance to succeed than most people in the world. I'd been given food and shelter and help to attend college, which I'd screwed up. I assumed these were his thoughts—that my shortcomings were an essential part of my being. That was our conclusion. While other people in the world suffered from more objective ills, I'd suffered from myself. Like my mother, I lacked "resilience." I couldn't disagree. A resilient man kept his emotions in check, a resilient man didn't collapse under pressure.

When I was younger, when we lived in the small town of Hallowell, I had thought of my father as a part of me. We didn't have much money while he worked for the state—balancing the checkbook every month was the most stressful time in the house—but I had felt that my father's capabilities in the world somehow protected me both in body and soul. He believed in hard work as the ballast of life. We'd always had food and shelter. I needed something else from him, but I didn't know what that was, and sitting just feet from him in his office I felt miles away. He was cocooned in his work and in his new marriage.

When he looked at me, I could see that I had become one of "them" to him. One of my mother's people. Just like my mother, in fact, a certain kind of woman. I opened my mouth and spoke of looking for a new job (without mentioning the one I'd just lost) and of going back to school to get my degree so I could find a real job, a career. I was too busy listening to what I thought he was thinking to pay attention to our actual conversation. I remember the tone of his voice, his eyes glancing off me, the shape and movement of his arms as he managed the papers and files on his desk. The smell of his pipe, which he clamped between his teeth even though he only smoked it outside and in the firm's roof garden. Before I knew what was happening, I was outside on the street looking at the fourth-floor windows of his corner office. He was up there, and I was down here. I needed a drink, I needed to smoke up, I needed one of my pills, even though all these had stopped working for me.

As I climbed Congress Street on the way back to my mother's apartment, it started to rain large cold drops. If the temperature dropped another few degrees, it would turn to sleet and snow. My head lowered into my shoulders as I started to shiver. The rain had soaked through my canvas jacket. I really needed a raincoat, I decided. As soon as I found a new job, I would buy a raincoat. When I reached the apartment, my mother would want to know where I'd been. I would lie—or I would try to lie—and say I'd been out for a walk, but she would see right through me. She would know I'd visited my father and she'd go on for an hour or more about how he had everything and she had nothing. "Why was that?" she'd want to know. People believed him, never her.

At the busy intersection between Congress and High across from the art museum, a woman stood on a concrete divider and pointed her finger at one driver after another as they passed. She wore a cotton skirt and a thin T-shirt, both soaked through, but she didn't seem bothered by the cold and wet. Her cheeks were red, her head held high. She was burning from the inside. When the cars coming up High stopped at a red light, she sauntered out in front of the drivers and started yelling at each one. "You," she said, "what are you looking at? And you! And you!" The light changed, and the drivers started to lean on their horns. Hands on her hips, she marched back and forth. I could tell that she had a lot more to say, and she was going to keep saying it.

As I walked up Congress Street through the rain, I felt as if I was losing an argument with myself even though I knew I was right. I should've turned left up Pine Street toward the apartment, but I was veering inland away from the bay. The person I thought of as Jason Brown was no longer in charge of where I was headed. Maybe I needed a raincoat right now, whether I had the money for one or not. Maybe I'd arc back toward downtown, walk into one of those shops on Exchange Street, put on a raincoat, and walk out. All I could think about was owning a raincoat until I saw the city bus speeding my way, and then all I could think as I left the curb and threw myself in the street was that now I wouldn't have to bother with a raincoat. Problem solved. The brakes shrieked, and a few feet in front of me, the bus halted. The hydraulic doors opened. Two people got off and walked up the sidewalk without even looking at me. I'd jumped too early and pitched myself in front of a bus stop. The bus driver leaning over the steering wheel and squinting at me was probably trying to decide if I had tripped or if I was, like the woman yelling at traffic lower on Congress Street, one of those people you just had to ignore. I stood and held his gaze for two beats, but there's a limit to what one can expect from a stranger. He threw the bus in gear and drove on down the street.

*

Soon after my failed run-in with the city bus, I bumped into my friend Dan outside Green Mountain Coffee Roasters. He'd recently gotten out of rehab for the second time but wasn't sober at the moment. I hadn't seen him in six months. We moved in together with some AA people he knew, and we started going to meetings. I got a job delivering pizza and called my new sponsor, George, every day because that's what he told me to do. I went to one or two meetings a day. I read the AA literature. It was like a cult, it seemed to me at the time, but I no longer cared. It was a cult that was willing to have me. I no longer had parents or a family. In AA I was among people who were at least as screwed up as I was. Without realizing it, I no longer wanted to die. After I hit the six-month mark, I had the unmistakable feeling at a meeting one night that a warm, tingling glow was moving through my veins from my toes to my head. Dan must have sensed something going on in me. He put his hand on my arm and pressed down as if I might lift off and float away. I had the feeling, not yet the thought, that I was being carried forward to something new. AA and the people I met there gave me the structure and community I needed to put one foot in front of the other. I returned to college, finished my degree, and started writing, all while attending AA and essentially living among AA people. There were no miraculous revelations, only tiny increments of progress.

Now, years later in Tucson, living with my mother again, I could feel myself beginning to orbit her reality, and it felt as if nothing had changed since she and I had lived in her apartment in Portland. I'd been sober for years, but it felt as if I might start drinking or using again at any moment.

Many of the redemption stories we read, particularly those about recovering addicts and drunks, trace a single arc from collapse to renewal, but, at least in my experience, the inner life does not follow a linear path. Many people who have to get sober, and especially those who get sober young (even following as brief and shallow a career with addiction as my own), seem to face more than one crisis. There is the crisis of breaking the habit of drinking and doing drugs. Most of us think we are free and clear once that habit is broken, but later there is the crisis of facing what led us to abuse alcohol and drugs at such a young age in the first place. Having lived through the first collapse, I had no interest in dealing with another one, or even knowing what it was about, but I had no choice. I would either move through this next stage, or I would circle back to where I'd started.

In Tucson I felt I almost had escaped my mother's fate, at least on the outside. By attending AA and working hard, I had finished college, worked as a teaching assistant to pay for graduate school, and started to publish. The outside was important to me. I'd always been afraid of ending up like my mother or some of her siblings. Living in some backwater with no real job or way to make a living. Time in jail and institutions. I didn't want to admit it, but the title "associate professor" served as a firewall in my mind between who I was and who they were. One of the ironies of devoting my energies to the "outside"—the side concerned with how I was seen by other people—was that I'd slowly stopped investing in people and in myself.

Since I'd returned from the therapy sessions at the Caron Foundation, where I had hoped that swinging foam bats at strangers would prove to be a shortcut to change, I had thought about finding an AA meeting, but I didn't really know anyone in AA in Tucson. I had one phone number I'd never used. Less than a year into our marriage, Amy and I were now "taking a break," which was easy to do while she lived a thousand miles away. I didn't know what taking a break meant, exactly, and lay in bed at night picturing her in bed with other men. This became the fantasy of my humiliation, which was more exciting than anything that was happening in my real life. Sometimes I plotted revenge in my mind by trysting with the barista (who didn't even know my name) at the café next to campus.

The goal of the addict is to remain numb—it certainly had been for me. When I was young, I'd felt too much, it seemed to me. I started drinking at age twelve and later found drugs as I chased a numbness that was euphoric and empowering at first and after ten years finally the last thing I wanted. It turned out that the habit of staying numb was much harder to kick than drinking and drugs. I'd found that the sober addict could find many ways to stay numb. I didn't realize at the time that staying numb was the surest way to worsen my depression, and I had no idea that making all women the repository of the emotions I never wanted to have was the best way to ensure I would never have a real relationship.

If you're numb, you're not in debilitating pain, but you're also not alive. If you go too long without feeling alive, you stop seeing the point of being alive. I was now so numb that alcohol and drugs promised to restore what they had originally stollen: a sense of feeling. This is one of the main reasons, of course, that so many addicts relapse and so many people who suffer from mental illness stop taking their meds. Sober and medicated, they don't feel like themselves. They want to feel alive again, even at the cost of returning to crisis number one.

*

A week after my mother moved in, I found a man standing on the other side of my metal fence looking at the padlock on the gate. He had left the engine of his Nissan running and stood, arms akimbo, in golf shirt and iron-free slacks. Shoes that shone without having to be shined. He held a piece of paper in his hand. I walked out to the front porch but didn't introduce myself.

"Do you live here?" he asked. I was back in one of my mother's stories. Even if I sometimes resisted playing my role, my mother had the uncanny ability to make me feel the exhilarating rush of being caught up in the rip current of her narrative: She could not be bothered by domestic concerns, she would not be troubled by details. Who wants to go to work every morning? Who wants to pay the bills and clean out the lint trap in the dryer? Not me! I thought. We do these things so we don't drive off the edge of a cliff. But the cliff did not trouble my mother. My mother preferred the cliff. Through the window of the front door, I saw her head bobbing around the kitchen.

"Does Susan Wende live here?" the guy on the other side of the fence asked. Clearly, he was the new owner of my mother's debt.

"Nope," I said. "I'm the only one who lives here."

"It says here that she reported this as her residence." He narrowed his eyes.

"Don't think so," I said.

"Do you know Susan Wende?"

"Never heard of her."

"She owes a lot of money, you know."

"It's America," I said.

He furrowed his brow, which made him look younger, not older. "Who are you?" the guy asked.

"Who are *you*?" I said, and we left it at that. He got in his Nissan and drove off.

And here we go, I thought.

It was my thirty-ninth birthday. That evening I was planning to celebrate the end of my youth by having supper with myself and later talking to my estranged wife on the phone.

My mother came onto the porch with the last of my cereal, and we fell into an argument about the absence of a washing machine. As the "landlord of this establishment," she felt I should buy a new machine, which was not really in my budget. And also, I told her, this was not an "establishment," and I was not a "landlord." She was a guest, not a tenant. I pointed to the building. "This," I said, "is my house and you are staying with me. If you were not staying with me, you would be unhoused."

"Aren't you fun?" she said. "I have plenty of places I could go."

"Where?" I said cruelly. "You have no money in the bank, a negative credit history. There's a man driving around in a Nissan right now looking to extract money from you."

"Good luck with that," she said and looked at the porch floor.

"You have a felony conviction—no one is going to rent to you in this town."

She winced.

"You're always right, aren't you? Are you pleased with yourself right now?"

I was restraining myself from starting the conversation we'd been having on and off for years—the subject of why she was here living with me in the first place. She refused to seek any kind of assistance or help and adamantly refused to discuss mental illness, at least in her own case. Other people's problems were fair game. She frequently speculated on my wife Amy's sanity. Whenever I brought up her own struggles, she admitted that she had sought psychiatric help when she was younger, after my sister was born, but she hadn't needed it since. In essence, she believed the narrative she had provided to the court: she was going through a rough time *right now* and just needed to get on her feet. I had offered to go with her to see a social worker, but the answer was no. She did offer to accompany Amy to a social worker because, in her mind, if anyone needed help it was Amy.

Much of the time my mother was coherent. One might think she was a little "off" after first meeting her. Then the delusions, paranoias, and magical thinking poked their heads out like gophers from their burrows. Many people who don't have family members or community members to help them seem to fall into a system that isn't designed to help them. Often that means incarceration or homelessness. I was certain that such an outcome would break my mother.

One old AA friend who had lived on the street and in prison in California for the last ten years had reported, in a moment of lucidity, that my offer of help would be wasted on him. He'd done too many drugs and lived with his voices and delusions for too long—he would never "make it back to the surface." It was just "too far to go." I was convinced that this would be true of my mother. Left to her own devices, she would be living down on the river fighting the coyotes for her second-hand sandwich. I'd seen it happen to people, I knew it could happen: in extreme circumstances, under extreme pressure, mental illness can metastasize beyond repair. I told myself I needed to prevent this from happening to my mother, but maybe I was already metastasizing, and my mother would be fine no matter what. My father had suggested as much to me on more than one occasion.

I told my mother I didn't want to eat supper with her that night. I needed to eat alone. I needed a break. I realized this was probably an extreme reaction, but I couldn't help it.

"Then I am calling APS," she said.

"APS?"

"The elder abuse hotline at Adult Protective Services." She picked up her cell phone, which I paid for. "And after I call APS, I'm calling my public defender."

I thought of my trip to the Caron Foundation, where the therapist had talked about the "abuse" (as he had called it) I had suffered at the hands of my mother as the origin story for all that was wrong with me. It was so appealing in its simplicity. That had caused this. If that hadn't happened, this wouldn't be happening. Solve this "problem" with my mother by unleashing my store of justified anger, and I would be free.

"I should call the elder abuse hotline," I said.

She looked stunned and slightly worried. The one time we had talked about those years when I was younger, she had lowered her head and said, "I was bad, I know that, I was bad."

"You can't call them," she said, "you're not an elder."

"And what are you going to report if you call them?" I said. "That I didn't invite you to my birthday party?"

"Yes, for starters."

"That's not elder abuse."

"Yes, it is! It upsets me."

"Look, that is *not* elder abuse. You're not being abused every time someone doesn't do what you want them to do."

I shuffled off to the kitchen wondering if she was right—maybe spending my birthday alone was a form of abuse. I sensed that she sensed me faltering; she followed me.

"You're yelling at me," she said. "That's elder abuse, too. I feel like you're always angry at me."

"I am not *yelling*." Now I was yelling. "I am not hitting you," I yelled.

"But you want to!"

Maybe I did want to hurt her. I didn't think I did, but I couldn't be sure. The people at Caron had indicated that I was perched atop a mountain of anger I didn't know what to do with. The only person I could imagine hurting was myself. "Jumping on the grenade," someone at Caron had called this instinct. Apparently, I needed to stop jumping on the grenade, but no one had outlined an alternative. Given that I was both the grenade and the person blown up by the grenade in this metaphor, I didn't see a way out.

"I can't be put on trial for what I want to do," I said. I knew this to be a true statement.

"We'll see about that." She gave me that look—pursed lips and raised brows. The look of a "mad" person. I couldn't step far enough outside myself to see that we were falling into the same dance. As a pair, my mother and I could not see beyond our history, our inherited and created roles as mother and son, female and male, victim and savior, savior and victim. I had assumed that if I just kept the outside of my life glued together, at any cost, the inside would follow. In the process I had created artificial bifurcations—outside vs. inside, he vs. she, my father's world vs. my mother's. To achieve the kind of outward success that would protect me from the chaos I associated with my mother and her family, I felt I had to avoid her and suppress anything that I associated with her. Now I had let her into my house, and she had nowhere to go.

I rushed out of the house and got in the car even though I didn't need to go anywhere. There's a certain kind of man who believes, in certain states of mind, that the world is populated by "idiots." Who drives around in his little red vintage Volkswagen shaking his head and talking to himself about all the "idiots." (The quotes in this case refer not only to my awareness of the term as dreadful and prejudicial but also to the fact that I could hear the word in my head as it had been said to my mother in her childhood and to me in my own.) Under too much stress I became the man who mumbled the word with the hope that he might stop hearing it. I went to Home Depot and bought a shovel. I didn't need a new shovel, but I wanted one. The old shovel had been made by idiots. I also bought a new handsaw. I felt the immediate need to perform manly labor. When I got back to the house, I sawed down a useless cocktail fruit tree one of the previous owners had planted. It was half dead anyway. Why would anyone plant a fruit tree that didn't produce fruit you could eat? Because it was cheaper than a real fruit tree, I assumed. Idiots. The tree collapsed in a cloud of dust. A useless tree. Spiky, ugly, shriveled fruit. The colossal stupidity of a fruitless fruit tree.

The fruitless fruit tree had to come down because the washing machine had to take its place next to the house. My mother was right, I needed to buy a washing machine, but not for her sake. The house was so small I had to put the washing machine outside. The house was a boat in a sea of dust, and I felt like an idiot for having bought it. I had bought it because it was "historic," and because I wanted to be part of "revitalizing" the neighborhood. By now I had figured out that this meant white people buying houses in what had been a brown neighborhood since the 1800s, so now the brown people couldn't afford to live here. I would have to build a shelter, something in the shape of a bus stop, to protect the washing machine

I couldn't afford in a house I couldn't afford in a neighborhood I should have left alone. The mortgage sucked up about half my salary.

I studied the spot where the fruitless fruit tree had been. I would set up some kind of gray-water system for the outflow of the washing machine. In other words, I'd let the hose spit the dirty water from the new machine right into the dirt backyard.

As my mother approached from around the side of the house, I had the strange feeling that I was in a film that captures ten years of a man's life in a few minutes. During those ten years, the man doesn't move from his metal porch chair. His cheeks sink, his hair recedes and grays, faint rings appear under his eyes. Otherwise, he is the same, sitting in the same position in the same clothes with the same expression.

"I have an idea," my mother said cautiously. "How much will the used washing machine cost that you are installing?"

I squinted at her. Usually, I could foresee what she was up to. "A used one? A hundred and fifty," I said.

She looked disappointed. "Is that all? Well, how about this? How about don't put in the washing machine, and we take $150 off of the money I owe you. Then you can take me out to dinner for your birthday."

The heat of the sun was like a tiny, soft jackhammer tapping my skull with a rubber point. (I had toppled the fruitless fruit tree, but I still had to remove the enormous stump. The washing machine *had* to go right here because the pipes in the house came close to the wall at exactly this point).

"Let's discuss this later," I said.

I started swinging the pickax into the ground in a circle around the stump. My chest hurt, I wheezed, I felt lightheaded. She was still standing there.

"Go away!" I said.

"You're scaring me now!" she said.

I kept swinging away at the roots, which clearly extended so deep that this would take me hours. When I felt like I was about to pass out, I dropped the pick, took out my phone, and went back to the dirt lot behind the house. Earlier, in my head, I had referred to it as a "backyard," but it wasn't a backyard. It was a stage set for a desert noir.

I dialed Amy's phone number because I needed to speak to someone else besides my mother. "I called your cell earlier," Amy said, "and got your mother, who said she wished I could see what 'we have done' with the flowers and vines out front. '*We've* been working so hard—it's too bad you can't come back to visit *us* in *our* house.' She thinks *she's* married to you. You shouldn't leave your cell phone lying around. She might try to sell it. You have a passcode, don't you?"

I had bought the house before Amy and I married, so I did sometimes refer to it as my house, which Amy often cited as an example of my patriarchal impulses. She was probably right, though Amy had never lived there and hadn't contributed to the house in any significant way. She didn't like the house, she had told me, and she didn't want to live there with me. Though our attraction, if you could call it that, now seemed based on mutual repulsion, this hadn't always been the case. She was the smartest person I'd ever met, and she had a brilliant literary mind. She was beautiful. In many ways we'd come from a similar background, which had bound us together at first. She'd grown up with an alcoholic father, I'd grown up with an alcoholic mother. Now we were in a circle of hell, yet I had no intention of trying to end it. In fact, I didn't feel I could live without her. I didn't see why we couldn't recapture the hope we'd felt at the beginning of our relationship. I truly believed that at any moment we would break through to the other side of our problems and stop rolling our eyes at each other.

I knew my relationship with women in general had been a series of disasters. Ever since I was a teenager, I'd found myself falling instantly in love with women I hardly knew. In some cases, as with Amy, I became emotionally dependent on them at more or less the same time I lost any attraction to them. I was attracted to women I didn't know or knew only in passing. They existed only as fantasies, which at this point was the only kind of intimacy I could bear. I knew it wasn't right. I didn't want to be this way. I felt ashamed, broken, and powerless to do anything about it. Amy had her own issues—otherwise she wouldn't have been with me—but we didn't know how to talk about ourselves to each other. I thought we just needed time to work it out.

I loved the way Amy now described my situation: "It's a disaster. And," she said, "you knew she was going to show up there, and you *knew* it was going to be a disaster." She was right, but that didn't make her Tiresias. She reminded me of the time we had brought my mother on a trip with us and she spent the whole time drunk and telling Amy she was a bad housekeeper. So clearly it was a kind of insanity on my part that I thought this—having her in the house, even as a guest—was somehow an okay idea. In my own defense, I'd never said it was a good idea. I just didn't see any choice.

"Choice. . . ." She let the word hang there on its own for me to consider in context.

I looked at the back of the house and tried to remember what I'd been thinking at the time I'd bought it. Chunks falling out of the plaster. Dirt and weeds. Water heater stuck on the back of the house. Why had I moved to this town, this state? My mother had just happened to be living here when I found this job. I had been offered another job, in another state, and I had turned it down. A coincidence, it had seemed at the time. Why was I always digging holes in the ground? No one else I worked with did these things.

Amy had recently started seeing a therapist. I was sure they spent the whole time together cataloguing my flaws.

When Amy asked if I was still there, I apologized for the situation. For my entire family, really, not just my mother. Of course, she was right—I shouldn't be in this mess. It was my fault. I asked her if she had any ideas? I could try to rent my mother an apartment, using my own money for the deposit and—but she had no furniture, so I'd have to buy the furniture (and now we were out of my budget). Then if anything went wrong, I'd be responsible for the lease. There was subsidized housing, but that took months or years of sitting on a waitlist.

"She should be in a group home or something," Amy said. "Can't you put her in one of those? Section 8?"

"I can't *put* her anywhere."

"I have no idea what you *should* do," Amy said, "but I do know what you *shouldn't* do. You shouldn't be living with your mother. I tell you this for your own sake."

Anything I could say to her at this point would confirm what I imagined to be one of her therapist's many reasons for not liking me, so I said I had to go and went back to work on the house. I moved a ladder, climbed, and started rewiring the overhead light on the porch. My mother, as a show of support, spent a few minutes raking the dirt in front of the house. I told her if she really wanted to help, she could pull out some of the weeds, but she said she wasn't about to do that. She would water the lemon tree after she had something to eat for lunch. She stood beneath me now looking up with her arms crossed.

"What did that wife of yours have to say?" she asked with air quotes around the word "wife."

"She's not my wife in quotes," I said. "Someday she's going to move back here."

"Good luck with that. Your wife doesn't need a place to live. *I* need a place to live. She should stay where she is, and I can stay here. You can, you know, visit prostitutes or whatever for your *needs*."

"Jesus," I said. I was trying to strip the ground wire with a Leatherman so I could hook up the new light fixture.

"Don't use that language with me. I'm your mother."

My hand slipped and the knife sliced through my thumb. I knew it was bad because it didn't hurt. By the time I reached the bottom step of the ladder, the blood was pouring down my arm onto my leg. My mother seemed to be delighted, not that I'd hurt myself, but that I had stopped working. She found it dull to watch me work and would rather we do something fun, like drive to the ER.

"That doesn't look good," she said, pointing at my hand. "Maybe I should call my friend JJ."

"Who's that? No, don't call JJ." I stared at the wound, feeling dizzy. I had no idea who JJ was, but my mother didn't hang out with healthcare professionals.

"He was a mechanic, before . . . but he can fix anything."

My mother knew a lot of people who'd been something or other and, for reasons that were not always clear, they now found themselves in the business of fixing anything for a small fee or permission to sleep in the garage. I seemed to be headed in that direction myself.

"I need to go to urgent care," I said. "And you're going to drive."

"I need to shower first. I can't go out like this." She pointed at her face.

I said she was not going to shower first, which led to a discussion of my telling her what to do. How I was just like my father. Always telling her what to do. Thank God she didn't have to put up with *him* anymore. Meanwhile, I was bleeding all over myself even though I'd taken a wad of paper towels and wrapped them around my thumb. Our argument continued into my car, where I gave her the keys, now covered in blood. I told her to hurry, and she told me that I'd always hated her. From the very beginning. Just like my sister. What would my sister and I do if we didn't have her to blame for everything?

She continued her narrative and gestured toward me, various houses, and the local homeless shelter as we drove down Seventeenth Street to Third Avenue and took a right, headed north. As we crossed over to the other side of town to the university area, I told her to shut the fuck up, which didn't help things at all. She couldn't believe and was sure none of my so-called "friends" (air quotes with both hands off the wheel), and especially my "wife" (again in air quotes), who all thought I was such a great guy, would be able to believe that I used that kind of language with my *mother*. Midway down the block, just past the army surplus store, I opened the door and rolled out of the car onto the pavement. I tumbled several times with my hands wrapped around my head and my elbows and knees scraping until I stopped against the curb. We'd been traveling less than ten miles an hour, but still. . . . Everything hurt—my head, my elbows, my shoulders, my knees, and, of course, my thumb. At least it was now quiet.

She must not have noticed my absence, at least not right away, because she kept driving with the passenger door wide open until she reached the stop sign. At this point I could easily imagine her wrestling the gearshift with two hands. One minute passed, two minutes. She was the worst driver I'd ever met. Reluctant to discover that I'd broken bones or worse, I didn't budge until I saw the reverse lights appear and the car start to move backwards toward my head.

*

At the urgent care, the nurse had used surgical glue to close the wound. After a few days, the skin pulled apart and it bled again. I sat at the kitchen table looking at the blood spreading into the paper towel I held pressed against the injury. The blood meant nothing. It would stop at some point, it seemed to me. The notable fact was that my thumb hurt. The more I stared at it, the more it hurt. My neck also ached from when I had wrenched it while diving out of the car. I might be imagining the pain in my neck, but not the throbbing thumb, and not the pain in my elbow, which still bore the scrapes from the pavement. I had a scrape on the back of my head that had bled into my shirt. It wouldn't be hard to talk a doctor into a week or ten days' worth of pills. Long enough to get my mother out of my house. Where to, I couldn't imagine. She had no money except a trickle of Social Security, and I didn't have much in savings. I would get her out somewhere, though. Then I would stop the pills. That was the lie I told myself. I knew it was a lie, but in this kind of situation it doesn't matter what you think you know or don't know. I didn't see how I could leave my own house. I imagined just walking away. My mother could stay in the house until it burned down or the bank took it. The place still needed more work. As an old house, it would always need more work. I glanced around the kitchen and spotted the silverware drawer. There were only two forks left. Recently, I'd noticed that kitchen items had vanished.

The changes were slow—fewer plates, the old saucepan missing. I was both aware that the kitchenware was vanishing and not aware. Somehow it was possible to feel surprised and not surprised at the same time.

My mother was seeing her probation officer, so I searched for the kitchenware. Eventually, I walked into the backyard and looked at the falling down garage, the chain link fence, and the broken vw bus belonging to Amy's father. I'd been borrowing it to move lumber when it suddenly stopped running. Now it lived in the backyard. The earth was disturbed around one of the wheels. As I walked toward the back of the van, it seemed to me as if I knew what I was going to find before I found it. Most of the silverware and all the pots and pans—all of them dirty from use—had been buried in shallow graves around one tire. Some of the larger pots were inside the van shoved under the backseat. I pulled on a partially visible handle and unearthed the saucepan covered with what looked like the desiccated remains of an alfredo sauce, now turning green.

Everything made sense—why there had been no dishes in the sink even though I knew my mother hated to do dishes. Why the drawers were a little emptier every day. Instead of washing the dishes, she'd been carrying them out back after she used them and burying them in the dirt with the shovel. The backyard consisted of a light dusting of sand over caliche that was as hard as cement. Amy's father, a geologist, had explained that caliche formed where no water had flowed for over ten thousand years. It would've taken my mother hours pecking away at the caliche with the shovel to bury what would've taken her minutes to wash. This realization, though interesting and illuminating, was no more surprising than the fact that my mother was living at my house while the woman I had married lived more than a thousand miles away. I felt I had no way out, though I knew this was a lie. I was busy trying to think my way out of the situation on my own, but I'd never been able to think my way out of feeling trapped before.

I was sitting on the porch one night with my mother when the phone rang. It was Amy. We talked regularly, usually about her classes and other students in her program, so it wasn't strange to hear from her. She liked to gossip about the other students, which seemed to draw us together. Tonight, her voice sounded different. She asked me how I was doing, which she never did. I didn't answer.

"Listen," she said, "I think it's time to say it's over. We're both young enough. We made a mistake, we can start over." She told me she'd met someone else, actually someone she'd known years ago, a woman, and they were going down to Mexico together for a trip. If I said anything at all, I wasn't aware of it. We had talked in the abstract about how our relationship was broken and always had been. One part of my brain knew the truth—that this outcome was inevitable and necessary—but the larger, dominant part of me was truly shocked. This kind of shock is no less real or powerful for being fictional. I stared at the receiver for a moment until I heard her voice again.

"This can't come as a surprise," she said, and I thought of the kitchenware in the backyard. The forks and spoons separated into different piles.

"Define 'surprise,'" I said, stood up in my socks, set the phone on the porch railing, and walked into the middle of the street. I didn't know what was happening—I was unstuck in time. Even though I could feel the heat from the tar rising into the soles of my feet, I wasn't in my body. I wasn't in any particular place but in all of the places my mother and I had lived at the same time—Arizona, upstate New York, Maine, California.

I had the notion, as I had many times before, that I was experiencing the loneliness and isolation of my own life and my mother's life combined, all of it collapsed into this moment. I felt sure she had been alone her whole life, in a childhood where her parents didn't love her, in a marriage where she didn't feel seen or understood, now in the desert where she had no one but me.

Shortly after my sister was born on my sixth birthday (a remarkable fact that had become commonplace), my mother disappeared for a while. I don't remember being told at the time where she went or why she was gone. My father must've stayed home from work for a few days, but I don't remember seeing him during the day. At some point, my grandmother, my father's mother, came to stay with us, though I only have one memory of her during that time: she was doing the dishes with her back to me. I wanted her to turn around, but for some reason, I couldn't speak. Late one night, I pulled on my mother's terrycloth robe, took a carving knife from the kitchen drawer, and walked down the street while my grandmother and father slept. I clutched the handle of the knife in my hand and walked five blocks the first night before turning around. On the second night, I walked six blocks. After a week, I worried I might not be able to find my way back. After the second week, I started carrying a coin, a silver quarter my father kept in his dresser, in my pocket. I had this idea that I would give it to someone if I needed help or if I needed to pay someone not to hurt me. With the coin in my pocket, I walked farther than I ever had before. The streetlights vanished, I didn't recognize the shapes of houses, and soon there was nothing but dark shadows.

I had reached the same place now, on the edge of darkness that concealed unknown territory. I was no more in charge of what would happen next than I was able to alter the earth's rotation. Hearing my name, I turned to face the front porch of my house where my mother was waving my phone in the air and yelling something I couldn't quite hear. She was standing on a distant shore.

"Come here right *now!*" she yelled louder, and I crossed back over the sidewalk. Each step felt like freefall. My body was forming a plan and had decided not to tell me about it. I wasn't going to stay here—that was over. This wasn't my house or city. The stars above belonged to other people. I needed everything to be quiet. I needed everything to stop.

On the porch I took the phone from my mother. It was my old friend George from Maine. I hadn't spoken to him for a month or so, and it seemed for a moment as if I had forgotten that he even existed. Somehow my mother had found his number and called him on my phone. There were two people who knew me—one of them on the phone, and one of them standing on the porch. I wasn't so much relieved as surprised.

"I've been talking to your mother, and here's what we're gonna do," he said and told me to sit down. I sat in the chair on the porch. "We're gonna talk, and depending on how that goes, we'll figure out what to do next."

I told him I was down at the bottom of the well again watching the world pass by far above. My mother and I were down here together, and we had no way of climbing out. George ignored me and said we were just going to keep talking. He knew me and was someone who cared about me—no brothers could have loved each other more—and, as we talked, the way I felt began to change slightly. I seemed to remember who I was.

Crime and Punishment

Whatever your brain tells you is real becomes real. The night I spoke with Amy on the phone about calling it quits, my mind told me I was twelve years old trapped all alone in my mother's world. There was no hope. I had no options. None of this was true, but I felt it was. The more I talked to George and reached out to people in AA in Tucson, the more this feeling lifted. It wasn't the first time I had learned that I couldn't trust my own mind, and it wouldn't be the last. If you can't trust yourself, who do you trust? In one way or another, I'd been asking myself this for years. If I stayed away from alcohol and drugs and took care of myself by seeking out people, I could mostly trust myself. But many people like my mother lived in a constant state of mistrust of herself and the world. Was she supposed to trust AA? she had asked me. She had pointed out rightly that many of the people in AA were just as damaged as she was. Could she trust professionals armed with therapeutic techniques and medications that only left her feeling broken and alienated from society?

I had often wondered if my mother suffered from certain illnesses or if she was a casualty of the system that had defined those illnesses in the first place—or both. Many people who suffer mentally do not easily fit into the categories outlined in the *Diagnostic Statistical Manual* (known in the psychiatric industry as the DSM-V). Even if they do, the categories themselves are the product of more than a century of cultural, racial and gender bias. In my grandparents' lifetime, terms like "idiot" and "moron," which I had used growing up (and had been used against me), had been weaponized against people in Maine who were removed from their communities and sent to the Maine School for the Feeble-Minded at Pineland. There had been a particular interest, around the turn of the century, in sterilizing young women and people of color who were deemed insane or feeble and at high risk of poisoning the genetic stock.

Under pressure, my mother lost touch with reality, but, unlike me, she'd never tried to harm herself. Unlike me, she'd never been prone to driving around in blackouts crashing into fire hydrants, trees, and snowbanks. I was the one with employment—for the moment—but it was not clear (as she had repeatedly pointed out) that I was in a position to judge her or that my reality was any less invented than hers. Was she supposed to trust me? She'd rather trust herself.

An older acquaintance from work told me he was retiring and needed someone to stay in his house across town while he was living out of the country. My mother could stay there, only three miles away. Now that her car was broken, she would have to take a bus to reach my house. A buffer. The place was furnished. I promised my friend I would look after his house and make a few repairs. I felt immediate relief, and for a while my mother left me alone. She didn't even call.

I went to AA meetings four or five times a week and spoke to people after the meetings. I spoke with George every other day. He repeatedly said to me, *Remember, you are not the hero of this story.* I nodded on the phone when he said this, but I had no idea what he was talking about. Part of me wanted to ask him to explain, but I didn't ask. I had a sense that hearing more about why I wasn't a hero would not yield short-term benefits.

While my mother had been staying with me, I'd stopped exercising and was living on fast food so I didn't have to see her at night. Now I was eating well and back to work. I'd been sober for over a decade, I was a teacher and an occasional writer, and I was taking steps to extricate myself from a marriage that hadn't functioned since the beginning. More importantly, I'd gotten my mother out of my house. I had no idea what lay in store for either one of us. She couldn't live at my friend's house forever.

With a few meetings under my belt and my mother living across town, I was feeling some respite. Part of me had come a long way from when I was twenty-one, but part of me was still twelve, the year I took my first drink. I understood that the purpose of the therapy at the Caron Foundation had been to help us go beyond talking about the past. Wielding our foam bats, we (the kind of people who washed up at Caron) were supposed to re-experience the past in a new context that would somehow free us of our orbits. It was all a paradox that still didn't make sense—if we failed to heal, we would forever cycle back to the territory of our damage, and in order to heal we had to cycle back there without drowning.

With modest doses of hope and despair, I started writing again. Making things up—inventing reality—had been essential to my survival since I was very young. I tried to work on my novel, which had seemed briefly interesting before my mother had arrived at my house but now seemed contrived and dull. I had a feeling for the language and the characters—the people—in the book, but I kept trying to force them to behave like employees of the novel. Like me, they were bad employees. Took too many breaks, wandered into the woods, stared into space. I recognized the artificiality of the problem (didn't they work for me?), yet I could do nothing about it except turn back to short stories. I felt at home in the story form in part because I thought of the story as a co-op rather than a company. The characters showed up to work in anarchy T-shirts and refused to take orders. No one was making money; the word "career" was never uttered.

On the side I was always taking notes and writing down anecdotes from my life with my mother. "Our book" was not something I spent much time on. It wasn't the book I was writing, it was the book I was living, and maybe for this reason I didn't take it seriously. My mother wanted to know who would play her in the movie version of her life. Part of the reason I couldn't invest in a story about my life with my mother was because of the subject. No one could possibly be interested in reading about my life. When I mentioned the book to my mother, she said, "Well," as if discussing a significant historical incident, "the story—our story—it needs to be told." When I asked her why, she didn't have an answer.

I had my mother to thank for giving me my first notebooks and encouraging me to fill them with scribbles. In junior high I followed threads in myself that unspooled a little at a time, and she always pushed me to keep at it even though the principal and some of my teachers worried that I lived in my own world and was a little "slow." She was angry that they had said this about me, but I knew it was true. At the end of every school year, all the classes had to take a test with blank dots that determined our track for the next year. We either ended up in the college-bound track or the beer-truck-driving track. I stared at each dot as if it were an eye blinking up at me. In the booklet, it was usually necessary to read a paragraph; between the paragraph and the options, I forgot the paragraph; between the options and the dots, I forgot the options. The difference between most of the options seemed irrelevant anyway; most of the answers seemed equally untrue, given that both the paragraph and the questions were completely uninteresting.

No one in a position of authority used the word "stupid," of course, even back in the eighties. But most people weren't tracking ADHD or dyslexia, either. The evidence against me had been building for years: I couldn't spell, I showed no aptitude for syntax or grammar, I read very slowly, I tested prehistorically low in math, I was usually distracted, and, most importantly, uninterested.

"You're special," my mother told me after eighth grade one day as she leaned over the kitchen table, her usual glass of Gallo in hand. "Special?" I said. The middle of Maine was not a place for nuances. It was possible, maybe, that I was stupid and special. My mother's claim and my belief in it was, like so many things, doubled-edged. On the one hand, if I hadn't believed what she had said about me, I never would've started writing, and if I hadn't continued to believe her over the years, I never would have kept at it. On the other hand, my writing would often focus on isolation and alienation (a turning inward), a state of mind, in my case, fueled by a sense that one is misunderstood—in other words, that one is not like other people. This conviction served as a bulwark against the conventional values in the world around me that I resented and was also a convenient excuse to become a selfish misfit.

My mother was supported in her thinking by my eighth-grade English teacher, Mr. Wally, who had circled a sentence in one of my essays where I had compared a woman walking across a room to a jellyfish drifting in the ocean. I had also filled a stack of notebooks with cartoons of gerbils, including scenes of mass gerbil suicide, gerbil religious hysteria, and gerbil war and love. The gerbils didn't even look like gerbils. They were stick figures with bubble heads and tall triangular ears. Sometimes they had feet, sometimes they didn't, depending on my mood. No one mentioned that they carried AK-47 rifles in a few cases. The obvious lack of artistic "accomplishment" in the drawings notwithstanding, Mr. Wally and my mother agreed that there was a certain joie de vivre in the carelessness of the work. Mr. Wally had been to Phillips Exeter Academy, for a short time anyway, and my mother took his word as gospel.

My mother embarked on a campaign in my family to convince my father and grandparents that I was special in some way that deserved attention. We were at my grandparents' house in Bath when my mother pressed her case. My grandfather removed the pipe from his mouth, squinted at me, and asked my mother (as if I weren't sitting right there) if she could explain in what way, exactly, I was so special.

"I don't know," my mother said after too long a pause. "That's just how I feel," my mother said. In speaking to a roomful of descendants of Puritan New England, she couldn't have said anything more damaging to our case.

I felt that my father and his family blamed my lack of acuity on my mother—on her influence or her genetics or both. My mother was only trying to get them to help me. At the time I appreciated her efforts more than I could express. Only now does it seem strange that she would have to campaign at all to persuade members of my own family to show concern for me. I didn't understand what it meant to be from a cold-pressed Puritanical family, not while I was immersed in one. Once, several years before my grandfather died in his nineties, I hugged him and told him I loved him. When I stepped back, he stood there staring at me for more than a minute until he said, "In this family we have never spoken like that." It wasn't an admonition, just an observation.

When I was in high school, my family moved to Portland, and my parents eventually split up. My mother and I lived with our dog Blondie and a cat named Attila the Hun in an underpriced fixer upper my parents had bought and planned to renovate. The house was entirely lime green—lime-green vinyl siding, lime-green tinsel wallpaper, lime-green paint on all the walls. Lime-green sinks and toilets. At some point, my father moved out. My father had a new job. He was busy. I rarely saw him or my sister. I lived in a dank apartment in the basement of the lime-green house. My mother lived upstairs, and we mostly avoided each other. My mother took dance classes, signed up to sell encyclopedias door-to-door, and talked about maybe becoming a real estate agent because she was good with people.

Whole chunks of time are missing from my memory of this period at the end of high school that involved car crashes, black-outs, stealing from stores and others to buy drugs and alcohol. My mother drank with me and my friends or drank alone at the kitchen table. I was stoned every day and drunk many days of the week. My mother encouraged me to write in a journal she had bought for me. Soon I turned from gerbils to stories. I sent one story to the *New Yorker* about Zen Buddhist sex addicts and was surprised, given my enduring faith in the "specialness" my mother had seen in me, that they never even wrote me back. I realized that my mother's faith in me was in no way connected to an assessment of my abilities, and in this sense it wasn't what my father, his family, or anyone else would have called "rational." Girlfriends came to stay with me in the basement. For a while a kid from school whose alcoholic father had beat him up stayed with me. People came and went from "Jason's basement," a kind of adolescent safehouse.

I started writing a one-act play about aliens from Benelia, a planet consisting entirely of friendly beings who are invaded by an unfriendly planet of moody, greedy, violent degenerates. The friendly planet Benelia sends a representative, in the guise of a human female, to a department store on earth to investigate people and bring back I didn't know what—a limited dose of cruelty?—that would help them to defend themselves. After conducting interviews with a minister, a soldier, an intellectual, and some shoppers, and after being roughed up by the cops, the friendly alien declares that it's better for her planet to perish than risk exposure to human nature. She dies in custody, on stage, of an airborne disease called Human Nature. My drama teacher let my friends and I produce the play.

I must have identified with the woman in my play—the alien— who'd landed on earth only to discover that she'd rather die than spend one more day in such a place. I didn't even know why I was writing the play. It seemed like something true, that was all. If a species of decent beings needed to defend themselves against a group of nasty beings to avoid extinction and their only chance of doing so was to become human, I was pretty sure they would choose extinction.

Not to write the play—not to make things up—amounted to giving up, to living with no definition, to sitting in the back seat and gazing out the window. The play itself, in its early stages, wasn't very good. I'd misspelled too many words. The first woman in my class I tried to convince to act in the play quit when she read the script because, she said, there were too many mistakes in the writing. After I had a friend help me clean up the spelling, I didn't think the play was half bad. I was somewhat aware of my dyslexia at this point (but completely unaware of ADHD, addiction, and depression). I didn't see what difference labels would make anyway. The world as I experienced it didn't care if you had a diagnosis.

I'd heard several parents of kids in my play murmur that the script was a bit "dark," a bit "grim." I thought I was stating the obvious.

After the opening night of *Benelia* in the student auditorium, a woman from the audience came up to me and placed her hand on my heart. She wore a cross around her neck. "I take pity on your soul," she said and walked away.

In a few short years I would be living with my mother in her tiny Fore Street apartment, working at the Cookie Mama, and ready to throw myself in front of a bus.

*

Once a week my mother took three buses from downtown Tucson to the Grant Road probation office where, she said, the more serious felons like herself were told that they had to get a job. She called her probation officer the Pug—a short-haired woman with no sense of humor about crime. Scenes between my mother and the Pug played in my head as I tried to fall asleep at night. She called my mother "ma'am." "Ma'am, you are a felon," to which my mother would snort, roll her eyes, and say, "Not really." According to my mother, this kind of talk drove the Pug nuts. There was no such thing as a "not real felon" or an "almost felon" in the Pug's world. A person was either a felon or not a felon. On this point, I had to agree. *You have committed a serious offense by stealing a $38,000 ring from a helpless old lady*, the Pug would admonish. *It was a mistake*, my mother would reply. The passive voice, the syntax of manipulation. The image of this round, turning-red Pug person with graying hair and one crooked tooth rose in my mind. I knew how the Pug felt. I felt for the Pug. On some level, I wanted the Pug to win, but I knew she wouldn't.

"What did she say this time?" I asked my mother one night over the phone.

"She told me I had to get a job!" my mother said. I heard her thunk her precooked chicken on the table. My mother loved nothing more than a chicken dinner.

"So what did you say?"

"I said what kind of job do you want me to get? Now that I'm a felon, I can't work in the school, I can't do care."

The Pug told my mother, "Then you'll have to take whatever you can get, lady."

My mother told the Pug, "I am old. I have been through enough. I am retired."

"Retired from what?" I asked. She hadn't put together a dozen years of full employment, for which she was justifiably proud.

"From all this." I imagined my mother pointing out the window. "Life."

The Pug told her, "You *have* to get a job. You have to pay restitution. That's what people in your situation do."

My mother told the Pug, "I can't afford to pay restitution, and besides, no one has ever paid restitution to *me*."

"It's hard to argue with that kind of logic," I said. I could picture the Pug as surely as if she were sitting in the room with me.

The Pug said, "You will be put in prison, lady."

My mother said, "Oh, no I won't."

I knew that at this moment the Pug would be disconcerted. Surely, she was used to people taking her threats seriously. I would've taken her threats seriously. Her threats were not idle; the consequences were real.

"Do you think I like not having enough money?" my mother asked the Pug. "No, I do not. Why do you think I stole that ring in the first place? That woman had no use for that ring."

"That's not the issue here," the Pug said.

"Isn't it?" my mother replied. "I think it is."

Less than a month later (a month in which my mother had been conspicuously silent), my mother called me up and said, "We would like to have you over for dinner."

"'We?'" I said. I thought of my friend who owned the house, but I knew he'd already left the country. Before she said another word, I was already laughing. I was busy grading papers, but I brushed them aside. I thought of Lily Briscoe and her relationship with Mr. Ramsay in *To the Lighthouse*. As Mr. Ramsay leaned over her painting, he was a menacing and paralyzing force, but once she saw him from a distance sailing in his small boat on the vast bay, heading toward the lighthouse, he lost all his power, and she became quite fond of him. The same was true for my mother. From across town, she didn't feel oppressive. Enough time had gone by that I was eager to catch up on the story. I sometimes had the illusion that my life was enlarged—made real or "special"—by becoming part of one of her stories. She liked to refer to the contribution she was making to the invention of "our" book.

"I can't wait for you to meet Steve," my mother said. "Steve is working on himself. He is in the process of piecing himself together." I'd heard this narrative from my mother before about animals, friends, men, herself. She told me she'd met Steve in front of the health food market on Fourth Street. Steve had a ten-speed with a rear basket that contained everything he owned. My mother had just come into "possession" of a house, and it so happened that Steve was "living rough" down on the Rillito River.

I arrived at their house with a bottle of lemonade and sparkling water. From the outside, the house looked the same as when my friend had lived there, but I now sensed a vibe coming off the stucco that filled me with anticipation. I didn't really believe in things like vibes, except when it came to my mother.

"Come in," said a man's voice when I knocked. I opened the door and there was my mother and a white-haired guy sitting on my professor friend's sofa, watching what seemed to be an old vhf documentary about ufos. They both held tall glasses full of some kind of murky liquid, and they both had wires stringing from their temples to a small electrical box. They turned their heads to look at me, and my mother detached the wires from her head. The guy, clearly irritated that I'd interrupted his show, stayed where he was and turned from me back to the screen. Here was the reason I had not heard from my mother recently.

"Steve," my mother whispered to him and rolled her eyes. Steve reluctantly removed the wires from his head and joined my mother. I asked if the wires and the electrical box were meant to enhance or deter communication with ufos or maybe had nothing to do with

UFOs at all? My mother laughed and smiled at me. For a moment we were coconspirators and cocreators in what was unfolding here, even though I doubted we were experiencing the same degree of ironic distance.

"This is Steve," my mother said. Steve shook my hand.

"Do you want a glass of colloidal silver?" Steve asked.

"No, thanks," I said. I must've been frowning because my mother smiled even harder.

"Steve's a pilot," my mother said.

"Was," Steve said.

"For Southwest Airlines," my mother said.

"That was before," Steve said, tilting his head sideways with his eyes closed.

"Before what?" I asked.

"Well," Steve said. "It's a long story."

Of course, it was. Daryl, my mother's last boyfriend, had sustained a traumatic brain injury. As a result, he'd spent his life cruising the US in an Airstream attending astrology conferences and waiting for the world to end.

Steve explained that a piece of a plane had fallen on his head, causing him to have a stroke, which temporarily cut off oxygen to his brain. He looked at me smiling.

"I see," I said. Two of my assumptions about this situation were now confirmed: Steve had moved into my professor friend's house, and he'd been hit on the head just like her previous boyfriend. Not only had he been hit on the head, but he was also "unhoused"—a term my mother had recently taught me. I was vaguely aware that my prejudices against men who'd been hit on the head stemmed in part from the number of symptoms I seemed to share with them. It's one thing to be aware of the hypocritical basis for one's prejudices and another thing to overcome them.

"Tell him about the time you were flying drugs for the cartel and you crash-landed in New Mexico," my mother said. "This is quite a story. Jason likes a good story."

Steve took a step back as if to assume a defensive posture. No doubt he knew the score here. The house where he now lived with my mother may not belong to me, but it was under my jurisdiction.

"That was a particular phase in my life," Steve said. His Texas accent peeked out.

"He crashed in the desert," my mother said, "and had to run and hide from the police and the FBI, who were flying overhead with helicopters looking for him. Three days, he hid out and they never found him. Can you believe that?" she asked me.

"I was living in Taos married to this woman and flying for a charter business," Steve said as if he were reading from a teleprompter.

"He was running drugs for the cartel," my mother said.

"It wasn't the best decision," Steve said and tilted his head to the side again.

"People make mistakes," my mother said.

"Yes, they do," Steve said and nodded. I nodded as well. We were in agreement on this point.

"Steve loves chocolate cake," my mother said and pointed toward the kitchen.

We all started nodding again. I hadn't seen her this content since long before she was picked up on a warrant sweep. If she had a home, maybe she'd be a completely different person. For a moment I experienced the thrill of having helped to orchestrate this transformation. In the story of my mother—in the story of she and I—I still believed (all evidence to the contrary) that I would be able to bring about her "recovery." She would join the rest of us in pursuit of a "normal" life by living in a house with a partner and having people over to supper for polite conversation. I didn't live this "normal" life—but I clung to the belief anyway.

"I'm licensed to do massage therapy," Steve said.

"That's great," I replied.

"Everyone thinks he's handsome," my mother said. "The women at the shelter really like him."

Now it was Steve's turn to roll his eyes. I took his susceptibility to vanity as a good sign. Proof of attachment to social norms.

"You're lucky," I said.

"It's nice not to be alone," my mother said and then led me outside. "Let's take a walk before dinner. There is something I need to talk with you about."

This phrase never signaled good news. When we reached the curb, she gestured back at the house.

"Did you know that drinking colloidal silver while administering a low electrical pulse will cure viruses, bacterial infection, and cell inflammation?" my mother said.

"So, you were electrocuting yourselves with those wires?"

"No, that's nonsense."

"But you were administering a low-level electric impulse to your brains?"

"Yes. You should talk to Steve about it."

We started walking down the street. Large houses with landscaping. My mother now lived in a much nicer neighborhood than I did.

"And I've been meaning to ask," she said, "did you know there were so many Jews living in this neighborhood?"

I stopped walking and glared at her. When she was with Daryl, she'd talked endlessly about my astral sign and how our lives were predetermined by the alignments of the stars. The new boyfriend Steve was probably an anti-Semite in addition to being a UFO nut. He was also probably racist, which meant she might start in on Amy's family, who were Hispanic.

"You know, the serious ones with black hats and the jackets," she said and pointed east.

"There is nothing wrong with being Jewish," I said.

"I didn't say there was," she said.

"Do you want to be like your stepfather, the Nazi? You're a *liberal*. You belong to all these justice groups and go to protests all the time, remember?"

"I'm nothing like my stepfather," she said, looking confused.

"You're starting to sound like him," I said sternly. Every time she found a new boyfriend, she started to orbit his personality until spending time with her was more like spending time with him.

When she didn't have a boyfriend, I sensed her orbiting me until I started to feel more like her than me.

I didn't like correcting her—I didn't even agree with the principle of playing that role—but I didn't know what else to do. My own warped personality might not be much better than Steve's, but what I'd decided to do—or what I told myself I was trying to do in my own paternalistic way—was encourage a kind of *All Things Considered* standard on my mother. I tried not to say anything that wouldn't come out of the mouth of Melissa Block or Michele Norris, and of course I routinely failed, usually by being mean.

"All right, all right," she said in capitulation. "You're right—as *usual.*" She rolled her eyes. Now that she had a new boyfriend, I would have to have this conversation at least once a week, maybe twice.

"Listen," my mother said, "I have to tell you what happened the other day."

"Oh, no."

"I didn't do anything! I was a victim!" She stomped her foot. "I was waiting for a bus over there on North Campbell Avenue. Because," she said, "you won't let me have a car."

I opened my mouth and was about to object to this logic but then decided it wasn't worth it. She didn't have a car because her car had broken, and she didn't have money to fix it.

So, she was at the bus stop, sitting upright with her purse in her lap. She had her cell phone in her pocket. She was headed to the grocery store. A guy in his twenties sat down next to her. He bounced his leg, tapping his heel on the sidewalk, and he kept looking over at her.

"'Hey lady,' this kid said, and he made this face at me. 'Hey lady, you got a dollar?' I told him I had a dollar but not for him."

"Why would you say that?" I said.

"Why should I give a dollar to every idiot I come across? I told him I only give dollars to people who deserve dollars."

"You do?"

"I do! So I said, 'I'm not giving *you* a dollar.' So he says to me: 'Why not? I need a dollar to ride the bus. I've got someone to see.'"

The kid rose to stand over my mother. He had a scraggly goatee and what my mother described as a rotted-out mouth, which I took to mean meth mouth. Common in Tucson. My mother shifted her purse behind her and prepared to be assaulted by this "cretin." Then "suddenly" a man in his late fifties came by.

"'Hey, lady,' the older guy said to me, 'is this kid bothering you?' I told him, 'Yes, he is. He's mugging me!'"

"But he wasn't mugging you."

"He may as well have been."

I briefly forgot about Steve and the colloidal silver and focused entirely on the kid at the bus stop. With someone else I might have started to wonder if the story was invented, but my mother didn't make these things up, not in the usual sense of that phrase. Her special talent lay in creating trouble where trouble would not otherwise occur. I thought I could see how this story was going, and I was worried about the kid. Things didn't look good for him. The kid protested that he was not mugging anyone. I could picture his face. His outrage. "I just asked her for a dollar!" The older guy told the kid to leave the old lady alone. Then the yelling started. The kid yelled for the old guy to mind his own fucking business. The old guy took a step forward and pointed his finger at the kid's face and said, "Kid, you better learn some manners pretty goddamned quick." The kid pushed the old guy in the chest, etc. The old guy briefly had the kid in a headlock, but that couldn't last. The kid turned the tables and hit the old guy in the face. My mother called 911 and told the operator that two men were trying to kill each other right in front of her. One was trying to steal her money and the other one was trying to save her life. The dispatcher asked where this was happening.

"Right in front of me!" my mother said. When she figured out what the dispatcher meant, my mother gave her the actual location. At this point the older guy went down and started to bleed all over the pavement.

"Give me the phone, lady!" the kid yelled.

"I am not giving you my phone," my mother replied, "and I am *not* giving you a dollar. I've given dollars to all kinds of people in this town, but not you. You don't deserve a dollar!"

"*Lady*." The kid shook his fist in front of my mother's face. "Did you call the police? Did you call the police on that phone?"

"Of course, I did. Why wouldn't I call the police? You're no good."

"All I wanted was a dollar."

"First, it's a dollar and then what comes next? It never ends."

My mother heard a siren. The kid must've heard it too because he took off across Campbell. The dispatcher was still on the line asking my mother what had happened.

"Did you hear that?" my mother said. "He's getting away." She grabbed her purse and ran across four lanes of traffic.

Indeed, I thought at this point in the story. My mother paused because she was out of breath. Yawning, she leaned against a Palo Verde tree and tilted her head so far back I was afraid she would fall over. I sat down at the base of the tree.

"Then what?" I said, impatient now for the story to continue.

"I was sure we were going to lose him," she said to me. "But the ghetto bird showed up, and I told the dispatcher woman I was in pursuit."

Up ahead my mother saw the perp run south along East Olsen. She relayed the information to the dispatcher who relayed the information to the helicopter who pursued the kid down Olsen Avenue. The police cruisers began to circle the neighborhood, and they actually caught the guy. From the moment he had shown up on the scene in the story, I'd been rooting for him. All he'd wanted was a dollar.

"I told the officer who interviewed me that I was a felon, but he didn't seem to care. He said I would have to testify. What do you think? Should I testify?"

My mother gave me the eye, one eyebrow raised, the other squinted. She was really asking whether she'd told the story well. That was all she really cared about—whether or not she'd hooked me. She could see me grinning as I shook my head, and now she was grinning, too.

*

My mother called and said she wanted to come over for dinner. She took the bus to my neighborhood, and I ordered a large pepperoni pizza for us. She gulped down an entire glass of water at the table and said she had news. I sat up.

Apparently, the police had asked her to testify about the kid who had mugged her at the bus stop. There'd been an actual court trial or a hearing. She had pointed to the kid and said, "Yes, that's him."

"Just like in the movies," she said. "It was my civic duty, don't you think?"

"Oh, yeah, who knows, he might've asked someone else for a dollar."

"So in the end they locked the guy up."

"Jesus, they did? Over a dollar? They didn't lock you up for $38,000."

"He's in the slammer as we speak."

"Is he white?"

"Yes, he's white, for Christ's sake. He was bothering me," my mother said. "And apparently he has a history of mental illness and of, you know, bothering people."

"You have a history of bothering people."

"Now, that's not fair. Everyone says how nice I am."

"Who?"

"I don't know. Go ask people."

"The Pug doesn't think you're nice."

"No, that's true. Speaking of the Pug, that's one of the reasons I wanted to see you," she said.

"What?" I said, truly worried now. Mention of the Pug caused me real stress because the Pug had the power to throw my mother back in jail. I didn't think I could stand it if my mother returned to jail for any length of time. They wouldn't know how to handle her there at all.

"When I got to the Pug's place last time, her people said I would no longer have to see the Pug—who's been treating me like a criminal."

"You *are* a criminal," I said in my serious voice.

"Not really. Anyway, this new woman, the Little Friend, came into the room. Actually, she wasn't little at all. She was the supervisor, the Big Boss. Someone who's actually had an education, so I liked her. I mean I didn't *like* her, but I could tolerate her. She was round just like the Pug. She said I probably wouldn't have to get a job—'no more of that,' she said. There was no point in the aesthetician job I'd been talking about because my crime was a 'victim crime,' and she said no spa would leave someone involved in a victim crime alone with someone to do their nails. I forgot to tell you that last week the Pug and I talked about me becoming an aesthetician. You know."

"You mean an *es*thetician."

"Yeah, a spa person, a person who spends all day in a spa around hot men. I could do a job like that. But now it turns out I can't because *my mistake* was a victim crime. So, what they told me they wanted me to do was take a test. A criminal test."

I didn't understand.

"I don't remember exactly what it was called. A criminal personality test—a test that tests the criminal mind. Because they didn't know what to do with me, they wanted me to take this test. And then I wouldn't have to see them anymore. I told them I couldn't just take a test. I would have to study."

Thinking I could see where this story was going, I sighed and leaned back. The Pug wanted rid of my mother, that was all. She didn't, probably, want to put my mother in jail. She just didn't want to listen to her anymore. Her stories weren't for everyone.

They ushered my mother into a room with no windows, a metal desk, and a stack of papers, and they told her that to transfer her to a lower grade probation office for "minor offenders," a facility closer to where she lived, she would first have to sit down and take the test. I wondered if tests like this had grown out of the fundamentally racist ideas proposed by Hans Eysenck, whose Jewish mother was murdered in a Nazi death camp. The theory of the criminal personality, commonly known as "a personality theory of offending," asserts that criminality is a function of a person's socialization and the balance of traits inherent to their central nervous system—what they had inherited from their parents. Certain personalities—people born with difficult temperaments—were hard to condition from the beginning. I was afraid of these ideas. If these traits were inherited, I was in trouble. My grandfather and my mother's brothers and sisters were almost all mentally ill, addicted, criminal, or all of the above.

"So, they left me in a room for a while, and I took their stupid test. Then they came back and took the test away from me and left me in the room again. I had to sit there alone even though it was lunch time, and I had asked for a chicken sandwich. Then she came back later—the Big Boss and the Pug—with no chicken sandwich."

"So how many people were talking to you?"

"Are you not listening? They told me there'd been some kind of *mistake* with my test. They were *not* happy. The Big Boss was all red like Ferdinand after he sits on the bee. Anyway, the Big Boss said I'd scored 'very high' on the test. The highest they'd seen in a while." She nodded.

"What does that mean?"

"*Exactly.* That's what I asked them, and they said out of a scale of one to ten, where ten is an axe murder, I guess, I'd scored an *eight.*"

The Big Boss got so angry that she started yelling and accusing my mother of messing with them on purpose—trying to make them look bad. She threatened, just as the Pug had, to send my mother to prison for a long, long time unless she took the test and the whole probation thing seriously. My mother claimed she had no idea what they were talking about. She'd taken their stupid test and now they were yelling at her.

"I'm a grandmother," my mother said to the Big Boss and the Pug and started to cry. A solid move on my mother's part. The Big Boss stopped ranting. It never pays to terrorize grandmothers. I knew this from experience.

"Boy, then they changed their tune," my mother said. "They went out into the hallway and talked with themselves."

When they came back, they told my mother that the reason she'd scored so poorly—so highly—on the criminal personality test was because she'd been under a lot of stress lately, due to her "mistake."

"I said that was right—it'd been very stressful being a felon. So they changed my score from eight out of ten to a two. You should have seen the looks on their faces," my mother said. "Too bad you weren't there."

＊

I couldn't understand at first why I was so upset to hear that the relationship between Steve and my mother was not flourishing. Steve enjoyed having a roof over his head, but he felt hemmed in living with my mother. Probably to gain some distance, Steve moved into the front room, while my mother stayed in the back room. Steve was also having trouble starting his new age business in massage and colloidal silver treatment—even in Tucson. Part of my interest in seeing their relationship last was clearly selfish. With Steve there, my mother spent less time focusing on me. But my reaction extended beyond my own interests. Much of her life since divorcing from my father had been spent alone. Both a symptom and a cause of her mental state, her isolation terrified me and broke my heart.

Without fully realizing what she was doing, she had assigned me the job when I was young of solving the problem of her loneliness. What she felt, I felt. I knew by now that I would always fail her because there had never been any possibility of success, and I would always feel guilty for having failed. My tendency to feel what she was feeling, or what I thought she was feeling, extended to other people I grew close to and was why I often found it so difficult to be close to people.

"That comes from me," she'd once said, speaking of my empathy. "That's what makes you special."

One morning Steve announced that it was time for him to move on. Using my credit card, my mother rented a car, packed all of Steve's things in the trunk, and they drove north toward Flagstaff. Steve knew of some people living in a camp in the middle of the woods on federal land. Some great people living off the grid. He called them "freelanders," which sounded to me a lot like freeloaders.

I felt as though I was with my mother on this trip, just as I'd often felt that I was with her when we were miles apart. I could smell the pinesap and feel the air cool as they rose in elevation north of Phoenix. Along the way, they visited Flagstaff, a town, they both agreed, where they might like to live someday.

Part of me hoped she would keep driving with Steve and vanish forever—then I would be free—but you can't really want what you can't imagine. I was sure that this was the way it would be for me: always on the verge of tipping toward her, always falling back.

They bought frozen yogurt. It was a clear afternoon, sixty degrees, the sun sinking into the tops of the tall pines. Steve had been given the mile marker on the highway where they should stop and the compass heading to guide him into the woods. When they reached the right number on the mile marker, my mother pulled over on the side of the highway and turned off the engine. Steve circled around to the trunk and pulled out his seventies-era, yellow frame pack, which he rested against the side of the car. My mother stepped out from behind the wheel. She was already crying. She couldn't help it. She wasn't saying goodbye to someone she had loved; she was losing someone she might've loved if circumstances had been different. Instead of loving each other, they had occupied the same life raft for a while, and now it was time to go their separate ways.

Standing outside the rental car, she and Steve hugged for a moment. Then he pulled away from her to shoulder his pack. He was not one for the long goodbye—he'd warned her of this. He walked with a slight limp, either from the accident when the plane wing fell on him, or his later car accident, or the cartel-related plane crash in New Mexico. He trudged slowly, in no hurry to reach his destination. If he didn't find the freelanders by nightfall, he'd set up his tent under a tree. My mother had packed him a sandwich and tucked it into his pack as a surprise, along with some of his favorite walnut brownies. The land rose up a hill toward the tree line. He turned and briefly waved. She waved back and kept waving long after he had vanished into the shadows of the pines.

A Chest of Drawers

Based on many years of collecting snippets, rumors, second- and third-hand stories, grimaces, and eye rolls, I had come to the conclusion that my mother's mother, a woman who never smiled unless she was being photographed, found my grandfather, Ed Keith, all teeth, strangely irresistible with his own car and plenty of reasons for everything he did and said and with reasons to back up his reasons. "Let me tell you," I was sure he was fond of saying in 1940. "You probably think you're something." His lips moved like he was about to sip something, his hand brushing back his hair as if he were afraid it might not be there (in a few years it wouldn't be). He talked through his talking, raising her up, letting her down. She was a college girl, the daughter of a man who owned a construction company. He must've seemed like a persistent but irritating thought, impossible to ignore; and she didn't even like him, not like the boys she'd known in Buffalo. Everything was practice with them. This one, my grandfather, when he spoke, it was like a coarse bark. "God! you are beautiful," he'd say, his eyes following her mouth as she spoke, reading her thoughts, seeing through her clothes. He talked as he drove, anticipating her objections before she could think of them, providing answers to questions she hadn't thought to ask. "I am a good prospect. I could get a job anywhere!" I am guessing that he was fond of repetitions of exclamations and sudden bursts of speed. She closed her eyes around the curves. He only wanted to sell: cars, himself, ideas based on the prospects of further sales, of aluminum and washing machines and the exponential growth of his charm, paid in dividends to her. The check was written, she had only to sign. The pattern of his message was simple: the same words and phrases, punctuated by a sigh or a flash of teeth or a look from the corner of his eye, which said, *you know what I'm thinking.* Instead of growing bored, she found herself drunk, no longer listening to his words, but surrounded by the rhythms of his speech, his gestures slowly becoming hers. His teeth were swallowed in his grimace, his voice like an engine turning over without starting. Before there was a choice to make, the choice was made, when my mother was conceived along with the Second World War.

My grandmother was a petite German woman who hated pets and had terrible taste in men. My grandfather, Ed, was a violent alcoholic. Her second husband, TJ, my mother's stepfather, was a Nazi (someone, anyway, who wished the Nazis had won). They both died of their own misery, my grandfather of suicide, my step-grandfather of a stroke after years of depression and agoraphobia relieved only by weekends spent researching his Aryan ancestry.

Following his divorce from my grandmother, my grandfather remarried and had four more children. My grandmother and her new husband had four more of their own. Among the nine children on both sides of the family there was a cult member, a pedophile (according to my mother), and an arsonist. A few of them spent time in prison and several of them were alcoholics.

After my mother's stepfather died, my grandmother was left alone in the rickety farmhouse where she'd raised a family. My aunt, who lived in a cabin at the back of the property with my uncle, announced that everything in the house would be sold, including the house, to pay for my grandmother's care. My mother, who had nothing from her childhood, told me that she wanted a chest that had been built by one of her German great-grandfathers. My aunt sent photographs of everything to Tucson, and my mother tried to determine which chest was the right one. None of the chests from the old farmhouse appeared remarkable. I pointed to a pine chest and asked if that was the right one.

"Yes, I-don't-know, maybe."

I knew from the description that the piece in question was in my grandmother's bedroom, and it was called the "Wichmann chest," after the immigrant ancestor who'd constructed it in his small fur-

A CHEST OF DRAWERS

92

niture shop. My mother called her sister and said we wanted the Wichmann chest. I couldn't hear the other side of the conversation.

"The one in the bedroom," my mother said.

"There are two in the bedroom," I said.

"There are two in the bedroom," my mother repeated. "She knows which one it is," she said over her shoulder to me. "And she wants a certified check by the day after tomorrow."

"My God," I said. "Fine." My mother and aunt hated each other. As far as I could tell, all of the people in my mother's family hated each other. My mother was what one might call a left winger—an anarchist, socialist, occupy-everything-burn-down-the-banks kind of person. I've shown her this line, and she didn't object to any of these categories, though some were clearly incompatible with each other. As far as I could tell, the rest of her family was as far to the right as you could go without ending the day in a stand-off with the FBI.

"Do we really know which dresser is the Wichmann dresser?" I said. "Or is your sister bullshitting us?"

"Oh, yes, we know. My stepfather used to talk about it. I don't know! It is the Wichmann one, okay? The nice one from that room."

My mother would have liked other things as well—the dining room table, the piano (that symbol of middle-class aspiration), the cupboard where her mother's holiday-use only dishes were kept. But we lived in Tucson, Arizona, and the farm was in Clarence, New York, outside of Buffalo where the family had once gathered for Christmas every year. I could barely afford the plane tickets to Buffalo, the rental car, and the price of the dresser. Before we left for the airport, my mother told her sister she also wanted a portrait of a chicken that hung in the mud room just inside the side entrance to the house. She didn't explain why she wanted the portrait of the chicken, except that it had belonged to her grandmother and that she wanted "a few pieces of the past." The price of the chicken: $50.

I understood—or thought I understood—that in making this journey, she wanted to salvage some evidence that she'd been loved. She needed to sit in front of her mother one last time, and she needed to carry that love in the guise of the chest and the chicken picture, back to Arizona. This was the way she had explained it to me, and I wanted her to feel this sense of well-being. I looked on the internet for what I could find on the maker of the chest, which wasn't much. John Henry Wichmann, a German immigrant, or the child of one, settled near Port Colborne, Ontario, and started a one-room furniture-making business in 1859. He also built coffins and was the town undertaker.

My grandmother had always seemed like a child (her family nickname had been Babe) who orbited the needs and strange obsessions of her second husband. There'd been no room for my mother, the leftover child of a mistake marriage and a constant reminder to her stepfather that someone had gotten there first.

I didn't want to visit Clarence or my grandmother, but I had my own reasons for going. Maybe by sifting through the trappings of the farm I could better understand my mother's childhood as a way of trying to better understand my own. I was certain that my mother had grown up without love, and this rendered my mother a mystery to me. I didn't understand how anyone who'd grown up without love could survive adolescence. I didn't see how anyone who'd grown up without love could be capable of the selfless love required of parents. The more I stared into the past, the less clearly I saw.

I hoped my mother and I could use this trip as a chance to speak about my childhood. We had touched on it here and there, but neither of us had discussed it since I had returned from the Caron Foundation even though she knew why I'd gone there. I wanted—or thought I needed—to believe that I had received love from her. Not just any kind of love—selfless love, the love of a parent for a child. I didn't know why the need was so strong, but I suspected it was connected to my wanting a family of my own. Now that I was over forty, divorced, and single, the idea of raising a child seemed remote. I wasn't sure why having a family was so important to me. Maybe I was afraid that my life would mean nothing, or maybe I was afraid of ending up alone. If most of my reasons for adding to the human race were based in fear, maybe I shouldn't have kids.

Given that most of the world's ills seemed to originate in fear, maybe my best plan was to do as little harm as possible.

If sanity is a function of being able to distinguish between what is real and what is fantasy and of knowing where the self begins and ends, it could be that I was no saner than my mother. Many mornings I woke in my house in Tucson convinced that I would be fired from my job that day even though there was no objective indication that I had anything to fear. My brain was like an old bicycle wheel that warped when I hit a pebble. I walked around with a mind that magnified news clips and emails into monstrous threats. These mental distortions always grew from the seeds of reality and stopped short of floating into the land of delusion.

Under duress my mother believed government agencies were stalking her, people in red shirts were gathering information on her movements, and that people she hadn't seen in twenty years were reading her mind from Maryland. With her old boyfriend Steve, she had dabbled in aliens. In part to ward off the spaceship—and just to get out of bed in the morning—I took prescribed medications, but I wouldn't touch anything that would get me high. That was the rule, and I didn't want to talk to doctors about my problems. I'd tried that. My mother wouldn't take any medication.

In the end, I didn't know how to judge some of the things my mother had done. In the *Nicomachean Ethics*, Aristotle limited crimes to acts of *free* transgression. Possibly it is more accurate to say that in my childhood I had endured a series of storms rather than a series of transgressions. In the end, it seems disingenuous to think so simplistically. There are degrees of mental illness, and degrees of free will, and they are constantly shifting both inside the individual and in a society that has pathologized characteristics that it deems undesirable. My mother lived in a world not designed for her. To what extent, I wondered, had I made the world a harder place for her to live in? To what extent did sickness live inside us? To what extent was our society sick and making us sick?

To write about myself for an audience other than myself has necessitated that I attempt to treat myself and my story objectively—as a subject of investigation. I have had to be willing to see what was in me, what was in my mother, and what has existed between us, which has meant, most importantly, being willing to see what I haven't wanted to see.

✳

As we boarded the plane, I pointed to my mother's seat three rows ahead.

"Where're you sitting?" she asked.

"Right here."

"We're not sitting together? That's too bad."

"It's okay. Couldn't be helped," I lied.

"Do you want to switch with me?" asked a woman.

After some shuffling, my mother joined me.

When we stopped in O'Hare, we learned that our flight to Buffalo had been canceled.

"Here we go," my mother said. "If we have to spend the night in Chicago, I want a free chicken dinner."

"Why stop there?" I said. "Why not demand a live chicken?"

"What the hell would I do with a live chicken?" my mother asked.

The desk agent watched us.

"We're flying across the country to pick up a picture of a chicken," I said, and my mother broke out laughing. The desk agent appeared confused.

"I can put you on a United flight this afternoon," she said.

"*United*—much better airline," my mother said and nodded.

"Well, the flight I'm putting you on is a jet, which is good because there is a blizzard in Buffalo, and you wouldn't want to go on the prop plane we had you on. Yours might be the last flight they let in before closing it down."

"There was no bad weather reported this morning," I said.

"I told you," my mother said. "Every time I fly to Buffalo, there's a blizzard."

"Lake effect," the attendant said and shrugged. "I found you both seats on the United flight, but you won't be sitting together."

"That's fine," I said and took the tickets.

After twenty minutes of walking across O'Hare, where the numbers and letters didn't seem to make any sense, we found the gate, only to discover that we had an hour and a half before the flight took off. The waiting area was only half full, but for some reason a woman a few years younger than my mother sat to our left. I looked at the woman: short, dyed reddish hair, small wire-rim glasses that seemed to pinch her face, and a plastic bag of food she'd brought from home. She was pale and cranky and probably Republican.

No one really wants to sit next to someone of the opposite political party, which made her decision to sit by us perplexing. I chalked it up to a lapse in judgment. She was probably exhausted from reconciling the many contradictions of her ridiculous belief system and from having to repress the obvious fact that the people she voted for manipulated her for their own personal gain. This was the reason it was so painful to sit next to Republicans—my own prejudices. My mind performed a cursory examination: the woman shopped at JCPenney, or someplace like that, worked in an office where she arranged appointments and performed feats of minor accounting, and had a couple of daughters married to overstuffed husbands who drove big trucks that never hauled anything. My mind would not shut up, and I felt guilty for riding the sugar high of liberal superiority—the not-so-secret vice, along with the five-dollar latte, of the NPR-class.

My mother dug through her purse, which usually contained everything but what she needed, and apparently failed to notice the woman next to us. I had a few minutes, maybe fewer, to avoid drama and a sense of culpability, which I also partially craved. My mother tilted her head the way caged birds do, when they want to use one of their side-view eyes. It was too late. The Republican sitting next to us had somehow caught her attention. My mother turned to me with the conspiratorial grin I knew all too well. One eyebrow raised, the other lowered; one side of her mouth curled up, the other curled downward; her chin pulled into her chest and a disturbing high-voltage malice flickered through her eyes. Here was the side of her I most loved and loathed, depending on whether she was enlisting me or blaming me for her troubles. Either way, she was most fully herself when she had identified, even briefly, an enemy force.

My mother always made things difficult for the people in charge—her father, stepfather, my father, her bosses, the government, the airlines, me. It didn't matter. Targets were interchangeable—she had issues with the people in charge. It was hard not to admire her for her maniacal resolve. Once convinced of her persecution, she would not listen to reason; she would deny the Arizona sky was blue.

She sat up straight and stuck her chin out. "Can you believe," she said loudly, "what is happening with the health-care bill in the Senate? The Republicans and their friends—like that Lieberman, in bed with all the insurance companies—are taking out every decent part of the bill so it's good for nobody but the *richies.*"

She glanced in the direction of the Republican and nodded at me.

I felt the same thrill I'd felt since childhood of joining her scheme to take down the man—the original "man" being her father and my father. I could enjoy this thrill because in Tucson my mother still lived across town in my friend's house and because I attended regular AA meetings.

"I know, I know," I said in my academic tone (which she loved, I could tell—the very music of legitimacy), "it is easy to get upset about all of these people like Sarah Palin." Here the woman next to me shot us a look, which I pretended to ignore.

"Yes," my mother said. "You know, the Rush Limbaughs, and—*frankly*—the entire Republican establishment, but you have to remember that they can't help it, really. They are an uneducated and simple people. Easy to manipulate."

"I see your point," I said with a solemn tone. The woman shifted in her seat, and my mother could barely conceal her glee. She pulled items from her purse and displayed them on the airport carpeting.

"You see," I said, "you and I know that the extreme right manipulates certain people. They play on their fears about terrorism and immigration and racism and communism—they play the abortion card—all to get elected. Then when they get into power, they steal the money from the uneducated middle-class and lower-class people who elected them. You know, those who are not rich who were tricked into voting for them. *You* know. Those people who own their own houses, but their trucks are more valuable than their houses. That is what the Republicans have been doing to these poor, pathetic people." At the word pathetic, the Republican woman cringed and emitted a gurgling sound. "Ever since Eisenhower warned us about the military industrial complex, the people running the Republican party know what they're doing—*they* are not stupid—but the people who vote Republican . . ."

The Republican woman gathered her carry-ons and stomped to the other side of the waiting area. I felt guilty for baiting her. I didn't have any desire to humiliate people who voted Republican. I didn't like the two-party system and belonged to a mass of people who couldn't stand any political party. I didn't think of myself as someone who enjoyed bullying people.

My mother maintained a straight, serious face for several minutes, her head bobbing up and down as if she were considering the merits of her own argument. "Remember my friend Steve?" she said.

How could I forget her last boyfriend?

"Remember that stuff he was talking about—the ionic disturbance towers, or whatever the government keeps up in Alaska, changing the course of the jet stream, and how the Republicans caused Katrina with it—you don't think that's true, do you?"

"No," I said, holding my hand forward as if there were a big NO sign painted on my palm. "No, that is *not* true."

＊

After a miserable night at a La Quinta, we picked up the rental car and drove toward my grandmother's house. By mistake, we first pulled into the driveway of my aunt's cabin, which was on a perpendicular road. We stopped at the clearing chopped out of the fir forest and stared at the rundown homemade "shack," as my mother called it, next to the maple syrup barn—one of my uncle's get-rich schemes that never worked out.

At my grandmother's house, my younger cousin, whom I hadn't seen since he was a child, stood guard, I assumed, to make sure we didn't steal anything. Almost everything that I remembered from when I was a child was gone. My grandmother sat in the living room amidst the stripped-down ruins of her life. A television six feet in front of her displayed a static picture of a Christmas tree. Christmas music blasted out of the small speaker. My grandmother stared at the screen and shrugged her shoulders to the music. Up down, up down, up down. We'd been told that she didn't know where she was.

My aunt said, "Mom this is *Jason*, your grandson. You remember *Jason*?"

My grandmother stopped bobbing to the music, looked up at me, and squinted. She knew exactly who I was.

"You look great," I said. She did, compared to what I'd expected. She rolled her eyes. "Look at that hair," I said. She had thick gray hair, not bad for ninety-four.

"It's the same hair," she said.

"It has been a long time," I said.

"Sure has," she said.

I smiled at her and she didn't smile back.

My aunt said, "And this is Susie. Remember Susie?"

To my alarm, my mother, with tears streaming down her face, touched my grandmother's cheek. My grandmother scowled—a look I'd seen on other people's faces who knew my mother, a look that said, "Sure, this fool." I felt immediately defensive of my mother. Why was the world always punishing her?

My mother once described a time when she had just turned seven and was given a litter of kittens for her birthday. She was always caring for some animal: bunnies, mice, pigs, dogs. One weekend, three weeks after her birthday, she had to leave the cats with her mother and stepfather because it was her allotted time to visit her father on his farm in New Hampshire. This was the coldest weekend of winter in upstate New York. When she came back, she found the box outside by the shed, kittens stiff as wood with their eyes frozen open. "They were making too much noise," her stepfather said. I frequently think of my mother looking at a box of dead kittens. She stood there until she'd stopped shaking. Then she walked inside.

"Susie lives in Arizona now," my aunt said.

"I should live in Arizona; I wouldn't be so damned cold," my grandmother said with surprising clarity and turned away from us. She knew exactly where she was, jammed in front of a TV Christmas tree outside of Buffalo as my aunt prepared to sell all of her belongings. My grandmother was in a circle of hell, but my mother seemed pleased, which made me want to scold her for being deluded. She had deserved more as a child, and now was her last chance to tell her mother that she had failed to protect her own child.

"My mother always defended us," my mother often said. Not when it was time for my mother to visit her father in New Hampshire, I'd once pointed out. Her father recognized no physical, sexual, or psychological borders. The scenes that had occurred in the small, square rooms of that colonial house had been alluded to repeatedly over the years, but I didn't have all of the details. I'd never asked about the kind of violence that breaks more than bones, the kind of violence that pervades the very air of a house like a poisonous gas. "Well," my mother said once, "my mother was newly remarried, and she didn't really want me around right then. She and my stepfather wanted to start a new family. And anyway. . . ." This was my point—a good parent didn't defend you only when it was convenient or only when they remembered to. Her mother also hadn't defended her from a stepfather who walked naked through the house, who repeatedly told her she was stupid and worthless and ugly.

Over the years I'd felt anger toward my mother because of our worst moments and because she couldn't seem to keep a job, fill out a form, pay her bills, or "deal" with life—so much anger that I sometimes felt like smashing myself into a wall. I couldn't even sit beside her on an airplane without feeling physical pain. If I had to spend more than a short time with her, I felt parts of my body and my psyche go numb. I felt it happening now.

Whenever my mother faced a challenge (balancing a checkbook, using a tool, operating any kind of device, or making a "rational" decision) that men had traditionally tackled, she hesitated and sometimes her hands shook. That she seemed to believe what she'd been told about herself filled me with rage at those men who'd forced these beliefs on her, rage at myself for being one of those men, and rage at myself for being like the mother who couldn't stand up to those men.

Where had all of this started—my grandmother, beaten by her first husband, who left him to marry a man who walked around naked praising the Nazis, only to send my mother back to visit her father on holidays, to a worse fate than what my grandmother had known? The mother who crossed a line with me, who suffered under years of my restrained rage? In the shadow of this history, questions of love and judgment seemed absurd. The love of a broken person is a broken kind of love; the roots of what damage us extend further back than we can see.

I remembered when I was twelve my mother's hand on my arm, on my hip, sending a jolt through my body. The way she looked at me, her face flushed, her eyes traveling from my face down to the floor, the smell of wine. These moments and others I couldn't bear to think about were like lightning strikes on a tree trunk—I had grown around the damage. Once people saw inside me, I was sure they would see my deformed shape.

Gazing at my grandmother sitting in her uncomfortable chair surrounded by the few things from her life that my aunt hadn't sold out from under her, I was hit by a familiar ache, the flipside of anger: feeling sorry for myself. I didn't like to admit I felt this way because I saw it as an embarrassment—a feeling that whispered, "You deserve more." In the plus and minus columns of life, I was far more fortunate than most people in the world. I knew this, but perspective is no antidote to self-pity. Feeling sorry for oneself isn't simply a symptom of self-indulgent delusion. The spirit and psyche can be wounded as physically as the body, and when these wounds do not heal, the self constricts and curls around the damage.

There is a moment, probably in anyone's life, when someone we know or don't know crosses a line and damages us, someone we love leaves or dies, or circumstances occur that threaten to destroy us or those we love, and maybe we look up and outward for help only to find nothing there. No community, no state system, no gods to offer solace. "The absurd is born," Camus said, "of this confrontation between the human need and the unreasonable silence of the world." We are set on a path we seem to have no choice but to follow, a state of being, as Camus described it, in which "this mind and this world strain against each other without being able to embrace each other." Under such strain, we do things we regret, things we wish we had not done.

My mother and I knew little of whatever her mother's people had suffered laboring on the Erie Canal or her biological father's people had suffered as coal miners in Mauch Chunk, in the heart of Pennsylvania coal country. Our troubles were private more than social or historical, except insofar as history lived in us and through us, as it certainly did. My mother once said that her father, as a boy, was beaten by his mother and told that she wished he had never been born. My mother's father and stepfather were responsible for what they'd done and who they were, but I'd come to see that—to some extent—some men were a creation of who they imagined women wanted them to be: the son, the father, the boyfriend, the husband. In one way or another, my mother had asked me to be all four, and in trying to be all four, I had set a pattern that destroyed my relationships with women and with myself.

As painful and consuming as my relationship with my mother had been, the pain of my father's absence was just as deep and trenchant. You can't reconcile with what isn't there. His father had been absent for him, I knew that, and my grandfather's father absent for him—on and on, I imagined, for generations.

The question that had occurred to me at the outset of our trip—whether my mother had been loved and whether I had as well—turned out to be the wrong question. The real question concerned our ability to forgive each other and ourselves. When I had returned from the intensive therapy sessions at the Caron Foundation, I had tried, off and on, to cut my mother out of my life. On a number of occasions, I had decided to cut her out of my heart only to discover that I couldn't without cutting out part of myself. My mother's burden, handed to her by her father and stepfather, was heavier than mine. If I could help her carry it without destroying myself, I would.

My grandmother's shoulders hunched to the beat of the music again as she hurled herself forward and back. I asked my cousin about the weather, about his job, and we made our way through the recession. We talked about how pretty it was outside the window, though I didn't really give a shit about what was happening outside the window. I mentioned that there used to be something in front of that window because I'd never known there was a window there.

"Yeah, there used to be something blocking that window," he said.

"A piece of furniture," I said and left it at that.

I had to go to the bathroom. I had sucked down two cups of coffee on the drive.

"Oh," he said. "I will show you where the bathroom is."

"That's okay," I said as I stood. "I remember where it is."

He followed me anyway, right to the door of the bathroom, as if he were a prison guard. He was obviously under strict instructions from my aunt to follow me everywhere I went. I seemed to remember my mother telling me that he worked in a Buffalo call center and that he had checked into rehab at age twelve. I could hear him clearing his throat outside the door as I pissed into the bowl, and, sure enough, there he was when I stepped out. My aunt in the next room could be the Republican we had sat next to in the airport, and this young man wearing the expression of a piece of French toast was her son. I wanted to ask him if he knew that his grandfather, my mother's stepfather, had been a Jew-hating Nazi who wished the Germans had won the war. During Christmas dinner, my grandfather would say, "I don't care what people think," as he reached for the goose. "I'm not the only one who thought we should've held back a little in the end and let the Nazis finish the job." For all I knew my cousin was a Jew-hating Nazi himself. If he was, I didn't want to know. I didn't want to be here.

My cousin and I stood facing each other until I could smell his breath. Coffee and Corn Flakes. I wondered if he wanted to beat the shit out of me. He looked like someone who wanted to beat the shit out of someone. I knew that look. It's one thing to talk about anger from a comfortable distance and another to feel the live wire of rage that seems to come from nowhere. A force more powerful than any human will. You don't have to act on it; all you have to do is feel it to know that your life is not entirely in your control.

My cousin took a step back. He was much younger than me. We hadn't grown up together and didn't really have a history.

"You want coffee?" he said.

"Yeah," I said, and we walked back to the parlor. He didn't get me the coffee, and we left it at that. I tapped my mother on the shoulder and said that it was time for us to go. She gave me a look that said, *Who are you to tell me when we go?* She was right. I was playing my role as the man again, a role I didn't want to play.

My aunt and my cousin escorted us through the house to the lower level where the Wichmann chest and the chicken portrait sat. I put my hand on the chest and said, "So this is the Wichmann chest, right?" My aunt's eyes widened, and she shrugged. My mother took a quick look at it and turned away. I'd traveled across the country, landed in a snowstorm, tossed and turned all night in a La Quinta, and spent a lot of money to pick up a chest that maybe was not made by some carpenter immigrant ancestor just arrived in Canada from Germany and that wasn't, as it turned out, all that attractive a piece of furniture. A small oak thing with a warped top and a broken pull. At least that's the way it shaped up in my mind. Like most of our reasons for doing the things we do, the chest of drawers was now beside the point.

My cousin and I carried the chest outside and shoved it into the rental car, a Ford Focus. It fit, with about an inch to spare, into the back seat. Once we were in the car, I turned to my mother and said, "Is this the Wichmann chest we have in back? Do you want to take another look at it?"

"What's the difference if it's the right one or not?" my mother said. "It's what we have in the car. I came out here to say goodbye to my mother. I probably won't see her again."

As we drove south toward New York City, I pictured my grandmother's eyes staring into my own as she strained to cross the years. I don't know what she saw in me, but when I looked at her, I saw only fear and malice. When my grandmother looked at my mother, I saw no sign of affection, no warmth whatsoever. When my mother reached out smiling to touch her mother's cheek, she must've been lying to herself. She was still lying to herself, I thought, as I glanced at her. Her shoulders were relaxed, her eyes closed, and she had a contented look on her face.

I wanted to tell her that her mother didn't care about her and never had. It was obvious, at least to me. Thankfully, I relented. It wasn't my business to tell her what she didn't want to hear—I had often made the mistake of thinking it was—and there was no reason for me to assume that I was right. We cling to what shreds of love we can find.

At the beginning of this trip, part of me hoped that she and I would reach a common understanding about the past, but I could see now that this wasn't going to happen. My mother and I were traveling the same road, but we were on different paths, finding our own truths.

"I'm sure your mother appreciated your coming," I said, and she smiled.

"I'm glad we took this trip together," she said. "I think it was a good thing for us to do."

Part 2

Control of Nature

If you're in love, there's nothing anyone can tell you. You're in a movie about yourself that no one else would want to see. Everything is going well for the main character. No plans based on feeling this way could possibly go wrong.

I met Nicola right before I left Tucson. We ran into each other at a drinking fountain in one of the university buildings. She had studied poetry and was teaching a class.

"Hey," she said when she finished drinking.

"Hey," I said.

This would become part of our history: "Remember when we both went to the fountain at the same time and said 'Hey' to each other? We were both thirsty at the same time (in Tucson)!" "What are the chances of that?"

Right after I met Nicola, I called my AA friend George in Maine and told him I was in love. It felt so *great*. Nicola was a five-foot-two, Italian-Irish, poet rock climber . . .

"Love is not a feeling," he grumbled. "It's a delusion. Are you going to meetings?" I was going to meetings.

"You're drunk," he said.

"I'm not drunk, I've been sober for. . . . Maybe I'm drunk on love. But so what?"

"You're drunk on something. And you're an absolute *nut*."

"This time I'm in *love*," I said.

"You're not fifteen," he said.

Because I was in love, I nodded (I was on the phone) and in my head said, *Okay, whatever, you're an old guy.*

It was impossible to believe anyone had ever felt so good before, though in fact I had a history of falling in love and quickly falling out of love, often in the same twenty-four-hour period. This is normal when you're thirteen, less acceptable when you're thirty-one, and embarrassing when you're in your forties. It was impossible to believe that this feeling would ever go away even though I knew that "love" amounted to a series of predictable though exciting physiological reactions followed by a prolonged hangover.

After a month together, the feeling had not abated. I bought Nicola a bike, and we pedaled through the desert. Love can seem to make the future unnecessary. A week, a month of feeling this way could be better than years without the feeling. While it lasted, the feeling itself was evidence that the world was good. Why wasn't everyone in love? They were busy was one theory. It was impossible to get anything done when you were in love.

When I was younger, the sight of anyone over forty acting as if they were in love was too much to bear. The horror of witnessing my parents go through their new beginnings in their forties (my mother on multiple occasions) had left me with the impression that love was a recurring virus for which there was no immunity.

Nicola and I thoroughly enjoyed lying in bed for hours, not lying in bed for hours, and taking long walks and eating healthy meals and talking about books we loved. We felt immensely lucky. My mother frequently told me I was fortunate, by which she meant that the world was cruel to her.

Within weeks of meeting Nicola, I had an intuition I wasn't all that familiar with—I could trust her. Either I'd never met someone I could trust like this before, or I hadn't wanted to. Probably a bit of both. In addition to loving her, I also really liked her. She didn't lash out at the world when she was afraid. Without fully understanding what this meant, exactly, I felt sure she was a good person, and this filled me with cautious optimism about myself. If I could fall for the right person and, more importantly, if she could fall for me, maybe I had changed. Maybe the result would be different this time.

I was also skeptical. Even if we're old enough to know better—and maybe especially if we are—there is an opiatic relief that accompanies falling in love. Any drug or anything that feels like a drug has the effect of focusing my attention on myself and on continuing the good feeling. If we're fortunate enough to fall for someone who falls back, we must try to see beyond the feelings, beyond our projections, beyond the hope that another person can change who we are and try to see who they are beneath the surface. I had no idea how to do any of that.

On our first date, Nicola arrived at the café on her ten speed with a giant edition of Carl Jung's *Red Book* bungee corded to the rack. I had tried and failed to read this book several times when I was younger, and the sight of its red cover the size of a serving tray evoked a nostalgia for a more passionate and hopeful version of myself. I was in trouble, I knew I was in trouble. I asked her what she hoped to find in the *Red Book*.

"To find?" she squinted and tilted her head. "I'm just curious. I've always been curious."

Was I curious, about anything? I wondered. No longer about the *Red Book*, but about Nicola, I was. I knew that my curiosity about Nicola was also a reawakened curiosity about myself. I wanted to know more. At the café, she ordered a bowl of granola, which was delivered dry with a carafe of milk. She drank the milk and after our conversation, she strapped the to-go box of untouched granola above the *Red Book* and rode off.

Nicola was baffled by the American financial system (which I took to be a sign of exceptional sanity), so she tried not to spend money; she hated stores, so she tried not to shop. She didn't care what we drove, she wanted to be outside as much as possible, she preferred the company of animals. She didn't know how to lie. I didn't think this last part could be true, so I waited to be disproved. But it was true. I was stunned, which in itself is an accurate description of being in love. Someone has hit you on the head, in just the right spot, and you feel dizzy. It's not a great idea to make major life decisions in this state of mind, but people do it all the time. The species depends on it.

The daughter of an Italian hairdresser named Roberto and an editor at Time-Life Books named Isabel who split after only a few years of marriage, Nicola was raised in both Washington, D.C., and Colorado. Her father had been a flamboyant raconteur who traded haircuts for free meals around town while her mother was controlled and bookish. Nicola's father had died when she was in her twenties, so I had to learn about him through her stories.

Roberto had come from a poor family in Carrara where his father etched people's names onto marble gravestones and his mother darned socks for people in the neighborhood. In his twenties, he left for the United States to work for a childhood friend who had opened a salon in DC. Because he didn't know English at first, he only traveled from the salon to the grocery store to his apartment. By the time he met Nicola's mother, he had perfected a broken English inflected with an alluring Italian accent, acquired an Alfa Romeo, and was doing Lauren Bacall's and Katherine Graham's hair.

Shortly after her parents divorced, Roberto moved out to Colorado from DC and opened a salon in a ski town. He sat on the bench in front of his shop with a pipe and his ponytail and said to women as they passed: "*Darling*, you are *beautiful*, but I can make you *more* beautiful." If a couple walked by, he said, "Ahh, where are your babies? You need to go home and make babies! Do you not know how? I can come over and show you how." He did Oprah Winfrey's hair; she tried to get him to cook lasagna for her, but he demurred. As he began to bald, he kept the ponytail, which flopped in the wind as he careened down the ski hill. In the summer when Nicola visited him, he drove her on pilgrimages to Ojai to the Krishnamurti retreat. On the weekends he and Nicola would watch boxing together and bet a dollar—or the dishes. He hated to do the dishes but loved to cook by throwing handfuls of ingredients that mostly landed in bowls, a slightly new mixture each time. When she was in college, he called her frequently and said, "I have two things to tell you: I won the lottery *and* your mother and I are getting back together." He cried on the phone when they had to say goodbye, he cried when she came to visit—he was always crying. Roberto was a character who lived in Nicola and lived with us in the stories she told.

Nicola and I went for long runs in the morning. At night I showed her my favorite Terrence Malick films and she showed me her favorite Andrei Tarkovsky films. We'd both grown up with family that had working class and educated backgrounds, and both of our families could be volatile and difficult. When I moved to Oregon, she stayed behind in Tucson for a short time, and we read poems to each other over the phone in the evenings before bed. Over the six months I spent alone in Eugene, I always expected Nicola to call and tell me she had made a mistake. The plan was for her to move to Eugene to join me so we could give our relationship a real try, but I never thought this would happen.

Possibly because my list of virtues was considerably shorter than hers, I paid attention the second time George told me that love was an action on behalf of another person, not a feeling. When Nicola finally did join me in Eugene, I knew I had better see beyond the delusion of love if I wanted things to last. I tried to think of what actions I could take for our relationship, for her. What may have seemed obvious to other people wasn't necessarily obvious to me, so I started small. I started with the dishes, forgot to do the dishes, and tried again. I moved on to doing a better job listening, and when I failed to listen, I tried again. What did she want? What did she want our lives to look like? Maybe love (for me at this point) meant learning to be less at the center, less in control, less fearful that things would go wrong and more of a person I couldn't yet imagine. I needed to unlearn myself in relation to someone else, to be shown by another, to not know what the future held. In other words, I had no idea.

One of the things I'd learned over the years is that you can only teach yourself what you already know. For everything else, you need other people. I wanted to learn from Nicola just as I had learned from George and others in and out of AA. I didn't want our relationship to go away, and it didn't. Being with her was unlike being with any of the other women I had known. The why of it hardly mattered at the time. Soon I was no longer afraid she would find out who I really was. She seemed to understand from the beginning that I came with a salvage title. She claimed she liked "characters," though she had yet to spend much time with my mother.

We got married in a field in Colorado. An environmentalist friend of ours, who had two young kids and had become a pastor of an internet church, married us. Friends and family from both sides sat on hay bales as my mother-in-law's corgi and my seven-year-old nephew walked down the aisle with the ring. After the ceremony, we feasted and danced under the stars. Nicola was gorgeous in an off-white, lace dress.

For the first time in many years, my father, mother, sister and I were in the same place at the same time. Over the years, I worried that my father, stepmother, and sister had developed a narrative that my mother and I were cut from the same cloth, both of us broken, mentally unstable, and codependent. As often happens in families, people define themselves in contrast to the relatives whose behavior frightens them or troubles them in some way. My father was *not* his ex-wife, my sister was *not* her mother, my stepmother was *not* the first wife. My sister and her family and my father and stepmother all lived on the east coast and went on vacations together. When I did see them, I often felt the way my mother said she felt when visiting her own family—like someone to be tolerated for short periods of time. Sentiments about one's place in complicated family dynamics are notoriously difficult to parse—it's hard to know, in many cases, if one is reacting to something in the moment or something buried in the past. It's easy to harden into a resentful stance and contribute to the problem; it's also easy to play the role a family needs you to play.

I was happy that they had come to the wedding. My mother and father talked to each other standing in the field. I didn't hear what they said, but I saw it happen. It looked civil, though my father seemed cagey, as if he were greeting a dog that was part wolf.

✳

In Eugene Nicola and I learned the pendulum swing of the arid summers and waterlogged winters. Despite the thick evergreen forests, the crashing surf and fog, and the rivers flowing like arteries through the state, this was not Maine. Like Maine, Oregon was fundamentally a poor state, but Oregon lacked the hardened north-of-Boston class structure. No one seemed to care about your college or your family in the way they had where I had grown up. The layers of history seemed closer to the surface in Oregon: the native culture had been forced out by what still in many places seemed like a makeshift world. Aside from the stalwart buildings of a campus cast to evoke the authority of the east coast, many parts of town still felt like a temporary camp filled with aging hippies, young hippies, professors, unhoused anarchists, organic farmers, pot growers, activists, rock climbers, heroin addicts, students driving Maseratis, nude sunburned septuagenarians on meth passed out in the middle of the street. Most of the people we met were from somewhere else and almost all of them planned on leaving soon.

Near an apartment where we first lived, a guy called "pole man" wandered the street late at night wielding a wooden spear with a knife taped to the end. He pounded on doors and windows with his spear and screamed for his mother to be released. He was convinced she was being held prisoner in one of the buildings. One night he took off all his clothes, set them in a pile in the middle of the street, poured lighter fluid on them, and set them ablaze. I wondered if his mother was hiding from him in one of the nearby apartments. On another night when Nicola was away visiting her mother, I was watching a movie in bed in my underwear when a guy in his fifties wandered into my bedroom and pulled open one of the dresser drawers. I had accidentally left the front door of our apartment unlocked. I flew out of bed as if someone had shocked me with a live wire and landed on my feet.

"I'm just here to pick up my underwear," the guy said. He wasn't a threat, he was baffled. I led him to the front door as he clutched a handful of my boxers.

"My girlfriend lives here," he said.

"Not anymore," I said and wished him luck.

Eugene was a place where people moved to escape the vise-grip of wherever they had grown up. It was a place where people felt free to start over. Maybe this was why many people treated the city itself as if it were a bus station. During my first year there, I biked to work. One day I stopped next to an upscale car at a stop light. The passenger window rolled down to reveal an attractive young woman who smiled pleasantly as she extended her Big Gulp soda, one quarter consumed. She held it over the ground next to me and released the container, which hit the ground and exploded all over my leg. The window rolled back up and the car sped toward campus.

Nicola and I adopted two Australian shepherd puppies, who we worried over as if they were our children. We drove all over the state with them. Oregon was by any measure the most physically beautiful place we had ever seen. The coastal beaches extended for miles. The waves towered over the pristine dunes where we ran with the dogs. Several times we saw large whales careening in the surf just offshore. Inland, the fir forests were thick and lush, the snow-capped mountains stood over the green valleys, and the high desert of eastern Oregon extended in long oceanic undulations for as far as we could see. If Eugene sometimes felt like a gathering of witnesses to the failure of the European experiment in North America, the state itself was wild and alive.

During my years working in Arizona, I had missed Maine and returned there every summer. Though my first ancestors in North America were from northern New England, I no longer felt like a New Englander. I hadn't felt like one growing up, either, as one rarely recognizes the air one breathes. Including the few years when I was very young and we lived out of state, after my father finished his education and before we moved to Hallowell, I had now lived "away" for more years than I had lived in Maine. I had arrived in a place without familial ties or a sense of community beyond AA.

In Maine the exodus from the state (and the fight over who belonged there) had been going on at least since Europeans had first arrived. Throughout much of the sixteen and seventeen hundreds, the territory that would become the State of Maine was a war zone as the Abenaki, Passamaquoddy, English, Scottish, French, Irish, and other groups fought over the land. My ancestors no doubt killed many people along the way. One Scottish great-grandparent named William Ross, who had come to Maine as a prisoner of the English, was dragged to Quebec twice and both times managed to return to farm his land in Alna with a musket strapped to his back. In the early 1800s many Maine farmers, tired of growing potatoes in shallow, rocky soil, fled to the rich land of Ohio. More still chased gold in California. After World War II, the paper industry in Maine began to crumble as globalization led to deindustrialization, and even more Mainers left.

Like most people in our immigrant nation, my mother's German ancestors came to America to seek opportunity and flee war and hunger. After years working farms and coal mines, her father's people left Pennsylvania in search of something better. Many in her mother's family fled the German communities in and around Buffalo when industry collapsed. Those who stayed behind had to make do with dwindling chances.

On the surface I had left Maine to seek opportunity, but on a deeper level I'd stayed away because I'd always had an idea of New England that cast my life as a failure. Now I was nostalgic for a past I'd never actually experienced. I longed for a connection to community that I had given up hope of ever finding. Only recently had I begun to suspect that many others in America felt the same way. We lived physically distant from the people and places we had known growing up, and we were psychologically distant from those we now lived among.

I had always enjoyed teaching, but in Eugene I started to feel as if I had turned a corner—the classroom felt more like a calling than a job. I'd been at it long enough that former students had started to publish books. Former undergraduates went on to study creative writing or become teachers, activists, lawyers, doctors, and a long list of other pursuits. On a good day, digging into a student story or a published story in the classroom, I had the feeling that we were partaking in a sacred activity, and the truth was that I had begun to feel a deepening sense of obligation to other people in the classroom and in life.

Whenever I shared with someone that I had gone without a drink for over twenty years, and that I had put together a number of years now without debilitating mental illness, they congratulated me as if I had won an award or scaled K-2. At these moments, I was reminded of my friend George's observation that when things go well (as they were for me now) we want to take credit, but the idea that we lift ourselves up is a seductive myth. We do nothing on our own. And several of the people I had known when I first got sober had not made it. My old roommate Roy, who had returned to Harlem and started shooting up again, was dead of Aids. Another friend was in prison in California. Another friend whose alcoholic father had beaten him and his mother through his whole childhood had survived a dozen suicide attempts and now spent part of every year in a psych ward. I had stumbled in life; they had fallen all the way to the bottom, and because they were up against too much—too much history, too much pain, and not enough help—they hadn't been able to climb out. For many, courage and strength would never be enough. The world would not give them a chance.

I hadn't thought about drinking in years, but I sometimes longed for the oblivion that drunkenness had provided. Even if we change, we are always also the people we used to be. Every time I went to the dentist, I secretly hoped to hear that I would need a root canal because of the Vicodin I would get on the other end. For me change was like walking next to your former self, always keeping an eye on him. *Stay where I can see you.*

If I hadn't persevered in my relationship with my mother, I would have remained numb to myself and to others. Now as a teacher and a member of a recovery community, I felt my mother with me as I tried to make a small difference in the lives of those who struggled to reach the surface. On some level, caring for others was the only way to care for myself. I kept an eye out for the students who felt out of place for whatever reason—the ones who were about to drop out, sometimes the ones who had already dropped out. They found their way to my office because they wanted to push beyond the classroom. Many of them wanted to be writers, whatever this might mean. I wasn't much help to students who wanted to write a genre bestseller, but those with a restless and wayward spirit became repeat customers. Developing something to offer the world, I tried to show them, was a pathway to well-being.

Nicola and I bought a small house on the hill above the university and worked overtime to fix it. I tore up shag, laid down wood floors, rebuilt the carpeted staircase with cherry, skim coated over the popcorn-finish drywall, and built a deck off our bedroom. I labored with the awareness that we were striving for what many people had striven for over time: a place to raise a family.

As always, my mother poked at me for striving—I was always trying to live the fancy life with the fancy job and the fancy house. I didn't think there was anything "fancy" about our house or my salary, but at the same time her criticism hit a bullseye in me. Owning a comfortable house in a nice neighborhood—I had dreamed of this my whole life, and now here we were. The house, though only thirteen hundred square feet and saddled with seventies-era bathrooms and kitchens, represented a level of safety, security, and separation from the chaos my mother's life embodied. As Nicola and I shuffled off to the Home Depot in our Subaru to pick up dry wall and two-by-fours instead of creating great art, I felt myself swept up in the flow of America's greatest myth of self-transformation through home makeover.

My mother admitted that her goal was to keep me humble and burden me with some degree of guilt for being an "elitist." It worked. I did feel guilty, but I also felt delight in our good fortune. Nicola and I savored our deliberations over what color to paint our bedroom.

On our hikes and walks, Nicola and I started to talk about becoming parents. We didn't have forever to think about it, and I was afraid of what it might mean. In speaking with Nicola about my apprehensions, I leaned on my own limitations by telling her that I might not be a good father. I really feared that there was something wrong with me that couldn't be fixed. Nicola had never seen me drinking or depressed. She had never met the man who dodged responsibility, careened into fights, drove headlong into fire hydrants, and wanted to curl up in a ball and hide. I was too old for the dramatic shenanigans of my youth, but I was fully capable of imploding on the couch. In short, when the subject of children arose, I was filled with fear about the future and all that could go wrong. She claimed to think I was courageous for standing up in front of students and running my mouth and for sending my scribblings out to editors to be rejected. To me nothing was more courageous than bringing a child into the world. Nothing could be more common, nothing could be more remarkable.

"Things can always go wrong," she said, and I knew she was talking about her father dying from injuries sustained in a car accident and her half-brother dying of a heroin overdose. She herself had struggled with depression, especially after her father's death. Her job didn't pay very well. I didn't make enough to support us all in the long run; she didn't want to rely on me anyway. At night before bed, we sat at the kitchen table and schemed about our future. We weren't young anymore, but we both felt a youthful restlessness. We were as hungry for life as kids in their twenties, and like overgrown kids we conceived of dreams that didn't quite make sense for two middle-aged people about to have a child: moving to Alaska to homestead, retraining me as a cabinet/furniture making carpenter (a persistent dream of mine), or, in Nicola's case, training as a helicopter pilot. One day we drove to a Coast Guard recruiting office and sat in the car talking about who would feed our baby while she flew into storms to rescue fishermen from sinking ships. I think we both knew that our dreams would evolve as soon as we were responsible for a new life.

On a good day, I thought I might be able to pass as a husband, a teacher, an AA member, but fatherhood seemed like something you couldn't fake. I thought of the trip my mother and I had taken to see her mother at the family farm in Clarence—the trip to pick up the chest of drawers and the chicken portrait that now sat in my mother's apartment. My mother, her mother, her father and stepfather, and whatever men came before them: the history stretched back farther than I could see. The surest way to keep that history from rearing its head was not to have children. It was hubris to think I could prevent the past from repeating.

When I thought about my mother's life in Tucson, I felt her unbearable loneliness. She had inherited a small amount of money from her mother, which, with my mother's consent, my sister and I had saved so we could dole it out to her on a monthly basis for her rent. She had a small apartment and just enough to meet her needs. On the phone she described people who floated in and out of her life. I heard several names repeat, but more often the names changed. The people she talked to lived closer to the margins than she did. People without a place to live, people in and out of jail or other institutions, people who walked the alleys rather than the streets to cross town because someone was looking for them. Or they thought someone was looking for them. My mother reported from a world where misfortune was rewarded with injustice and just as often injustice was treated as misfortune.

She joined the Bus Riders Union to fight the city's investment in a short-run streetcar extending from the university to downtown—an expensive stunt that would mean the closure of regular bus lines. She would frequently give dollar bills to people who said they were starving. She would lend them the car I had paid to repair or anything she owned. She left the door to her place unlocked and sometimes wide open while she took walks with her cat. I knew people were taking advantage of her, and there was nothing I could do about it from a distance.

When she asked me for extra money, over and above her rent, either around the holidays or because she needed to go to the dentist, I grumbled because I knew she wasn't careful with the money she had. When I went to visit, I found her place filthy. I usually had to clean hundreds of dollars of rotten, high-end gourmet food out of the refrigerator. Food she hadn't eaten because she'd failed to cook; instead, she'd stopped by a restaurant with her dentist money.

I tired of trying to explain to her why this was no way to live. In my mind, life had stood still for my mother while mine had steadily improved. She lived, it seemed to me, like someone who had never been taught how to live, who had been taught that they didn't deserve any better, like someone who had given up, who was fighting a long battle with mental illness. There is such a thing as a living suicide; someone can be alive but no longer living. She was still sober—and, to my surprise, she'd even given up smoking—but she repeatedly put herself in crisis, both financially and emotionally, and needed to be bailed out. Unpaid rent, utilities, bills. Fights with her friends and boyfriends that led to emotional collapses and my flying to see her. Each time she had a crisis, I felt the gravitational pull to try to fix the problem from far away. My father and sister told me I should get more distance from her to protect myself, let her sink or swim on her own. I wanted her to be part of what I saw as a saner, calmer, orderly, and financially stable life—the one I was trying to build in Oregon. It never occurred to me that she didn't want to change. She just wanted me back in her story.

I tried not to think about how she filled her hours. She walked around town or sat in front of her apartment making connections that never seemed to last. She spent days huddled with the Occupy people in Tucson and was even interviewed by the local paper about her views on the movement. She immediately assumed the role of spokesperson and railed against the one percent, the New York bankers. For the most part, though, she sat alone with her cat in her dirty place and read or watched TV. She called me one day when she had finished the entire Border Trilogy by Cormac McCarthy, a contemporary literary tome, and wondered what I thought about this hallucinogenic vision of the southwest. I told her I didn't have any immediate wisdom because I had yet to finish the whole trilogy. She told me I should at least read *Blood Meridian*. I told her I had read that one.

"Well, I should think so. I like the Judge," she said, speaking of the main character, a Nietzschean *ubermensch*. "He is someone I would like to speak to."

Indeed, I told her, that was a conversation I would pay to witness. I was sure the Judge would have met his match.

*

Nicola, who had spent little time with my mother, thought moving her to Eugene was a good idea. In a twist of logic that I still can't unravel, the decision to move my mother to Eugene led me to embrace the idea of having a child. Nicola pointed out that my mother could spend more time with the family and maybe even help out with the baby. "Yes," I said, "that's true." I believed every word she said on the matter even though her predictions with regard to my mother were based on a lack of understanding. It wasn't that different from a nonalcoholic saying to an alcoholic, "You can have one beer, can't you? Surely one won't hurt you?" Nothing could sound more reasonable to the alcoholic.

I told my mother that I would arrange everything. All she had to do was drive her car with Attila the Hun III, but every time she stopped at a hotel, the cat managed to escape and hide somewhere in the room or the gym or the buffet. From Arizona to Nevada to California and Oregon, entire hotel staffs repeatedly mobilized to search for "Tillie." By the time they arrived, both my mother's hair and the cat's fur were standing on end.

I'd found my mother an apartment near the river park three miles from our house. It was too large, but it was inexpensive for Eugene. She liked the neighborhood, and she liked walking in the park. I tried to bring my mother into our lives by having her to meals at our place with Nicola. Unfortunately, we soon discovered that my mother couldn't spend time with Nicola without lashing out. We had tried to make it work several times, but my mother would rant, calling Nicola a "delicate flower" who was "damaged and sick." Nicola was a control freak, Nicola hated the homeless, Nicola was a monstrous ice princess, Nicola was a "capitalist one percenter!"

Once while she was over at our place, my mother looked at Nicola and back to me. "You have no idea what she says to me when you're not around," my mother whispered and raised her eyebrows.

"I'm standing right *here*," Nicola said.

"That woman rules your life!" my mother shouted when we were in the car driving back to her apartment. "You need to stand up for me and smash her down."

My mother was clearly threatened by Nicola. Everything I did for my wife I should be doing for my mother. As a result, I had to keep them apart, which meant I had to meet my mother for coffee. My mother loved action movies, so we spent time at the Cineplex. I tried to avoid her apartment.

After several months passed without my mother complaining to me about Nicola, she asked us if we would come to her apartment to have cake. Nicola and I agreed. No occasion. She wanted us to eat cake. My mother knew we were coming—she'd invited us.

The air was different around my mother's apartment, down by the river, near the homeless camps. Nicola claimed she had no idea what I was talking about and that this was a case (not the first one) of my "imagination working overtime."

Normally, I smelled nothing, least of all myself, but coming into my mother's radius, my nose became a dosimeter of malodorous disturbances. I knew something was wrong the moment I punched the code into the front door (541, the local area code) and Nicola and I entered the small lobby. My mother liked old buildings, so I had found an old apartment building, but as we stood in the entranceway, I decided that people shouldn't live in hundred-year-old buildings—especially apartment buildings—in mizzling climates. I looked down at the old wet carpeting under my feet. Brown had been a good choice, except it had been stretched over the even older gray carpeting. A large hole had worn through both layers of carpeting to reveal the wet planks beneath. As usual, we had Franny and Cheever, our two shepherds, with us, and they too were focused on the hole in the carpet. I stared down and thought, I never, ever, want to live in an old house again. I thought of the 1780s house where I'd grown up. The smoke-billowing woodstove and wood-burning furnace, the toothbrushes frozen to the wall of the bathroom, the pipes bursting, the asbestos siding on the south side. Wide pine boards, leaded glass from India, horsehair plaster—a geology of charming ills. In a new house, one lived, for the most part, with only the latest flawed ideas.

"We should leave," I said to Nicola.

"What're you talking about?" she said.

"Don't you smell that?" She was about to knock on my mother's door, but she paused and sniffed.

"Mold?"

My mother threw open the door and welcomed us inside. Except we couldn't go more than eight to ten inches past her smile. Tillie sat on a dining table, perched above a sea of garbage. But for a narrow walkway to the table where the glorious carrot cake rested with burning candles, the mounds of garbage bags covered the entire floor. Not recycling, as one might hope, but food scraps, used cat litter, mountains of paper towels rising beyond the windowsill (she'd borrowed money from me the week before to buy more paper towels), plastic bottles, cat food cans that hadn't been washed out. A biohazard. I covered my nose and locked eyes with the cat. "I'm sorry," I said in my mind to the cat. "I've been busy lately. I took my eye off the ball . . . ? I'm sorry, sorry, sorry."

"What's the matter?" my mother said. At this point I noticed that she was wearing a red-and-green wool Christmas dress with what looked like a reindeer on the front. Nicola grabbed my arm. We stood for a moment, frozen. A pin had been removed from a psychic grenade in my chest.

"I have some leftover meatloaf," my mother said, "if you want to eat before the cake."

"We just ate," Nicola said. She sounded a lot like Siri.

"And now what we want is to take you out for dessert," I said in what sounded like the "Danger Will Robinson" voice of the robot from *Lost in Space*, a TV show from my childhood. All the implausible details of that show were coming back to me. I headed for the front door with Franny and Cheever and left Nicola to deal with my mother.

In the Subaru, I turned on *Marketplace* and initiated the process of disassociation. I loved the voice of the host, Kai Ryssdal. Kai's voice represented a world that confronted and eventually conquered all challenges. He played trombones if the market went down, trumpets if the market went up. I wanted to live in that world. I wanted to be part of a market.

✳

The following week I was in my office at work trying to print out a comment for a student paper when the phone rang.

"May I speak to Jason Brown?"

What I wanted to say was, "Jason Brown has entered the witness protection program and is living under an assumed name in an undisclosed location."

It was the new property management company handling my mother's rental. My name was on the lease, a fact I'd chosen to forget. I recognized the voice—Bridget from my AA home group.

I told her I was sorry. "Sorry for what?" she asked. "For this whole thing," I said, "whatever it is we are about to discuss." She explained that the owner of the building had managed the property himself until—well, frankly, until he rented to my mother. The owner had been getting older, and my mother had proved too much for him. Somehow my mother had convinced him to give her his phone number. Now she called him all the time about strange smells and noises, loud neighbors, social problems that didn't just affect their street but, if you thought about it, the entire region. Mainly she called him because she couldn't pay the rent even though I had given her the money to do so. She had pushed him over the edge. "Yeah," I said, "not surprising." Finally settling on the crisis at hand, Bridget wondered if I had seen the bathroom in the apartment lately. "The bathroom?" I said. "No. I make a point of not seeing the bathroom."

"Well," Bridget said, "the thing is that the bathroom is destroyed, basically. They are not sure how much they can save. They have to get a team in there to assess."

"A *team*? A team of what?"

"I don't know. That's what the cleaners said. They don't feel comfortable going in there without the proper gear, I guess. I hate to say this, but there was, you know, sewage everywhere—in the sink, the tub. I don't think the toilet was being used for a while, after it stopped working probably some time ago. But that's just what they could see from outside the bathroom. We'll know more once we can get inside."

Silence on my end. I'd gone down the street in my mind. "You've spoken to my mother about this?"

"We did, I mean we tried to. I don't think—well, I don't think she likes me. We also mentioned the problem in the living room and kitchen with all the bags." I told her I'd been working on the bag problem, which meant, essentially, that I'd done nothing about the bag problem but worry about it. In addition to the bags, all the carpets were soaked with urine, the closets were full of cat shit, and—mysteriously—it looked as if there'd been some kind of infestation of fruit flies or fleas that had been sprayed with something that had shellacked them to every surface of the apartment.

When I got off the phone with Bridget, I immediately called my mother, who announced that she was enjoying some grapes at that moment. Sitting on the front steps enjoying some grapes.

"That's nice," I said, "and did you know you are about to be evicted?"

"What? No! What're you talking about? That woman Bridget? She's awful. She says she knows you."

"She does."

"She won't give me landlord Jerry's new phone number. She tells me Jerry is on vacation, which I know is a lie."

"It could be that 'landlord Jerry' doesn't want to talk to you. That's why we have Bridget, and she is serious. We—and by *we* I mean *I*—am going to have to pay to maybe rebuild the bathroom and who knows what else."

My mother guffawed. "That's nonsense. It's a little dirty. I need to buy a mop and a new sponge. I really need a new sponge. Then I'll get started on it."

"If you are not physically able to clean, you need to tell me."

"There is nothing wrong with me."

"The guys who looked at the place had to leave so they can come back later with hazmat suits, and the amount of garbage on your floor would overflow a dumpster. Maybe . . . do you think it's time to talk about living somewhere with some help. Assisted living?"

"You could use some help with that wife of yours, but good luck finding a place that will do that."

"I'm not talking about *me*."

"*Me?*" she said. "I don't need help. Why don't I come over to take care of the dogs while you and Nicola go out to dinner," my mother said. "You clearly need to relax."

I knew I was facing the same old confusion. I didn't wonder what she was doing wrong, I wondered what I had done wrong. I had moved her into the wrong apartment, I wasn't spending enough time with her. Or possibly, given the level of despair and illness manifested in the destruction to the apartment, she should be in an institution, assisted living, or a group home. As always, though, she wasn't going to accept help or any insinuation that something was wrong. Also, I couldn't afford to pay to have her in some private institution.

"My friend Jacob dropped off his cat Kiwi," my mother said.

"Wait, who's Jacob?" I knew she was changing the subject on purpose, and I didn't have the energy to resist. Also, I wanted to change the subject as much as she did.

"He's a member of my group." She meant her political group, the Go Bernies. "He lives in an RV that doesn't work, which makes him unhappy. I'm the only person allowed to take care of Kiwi, which is happening more and more often these days."

"Why is that?"

"Well, last night it was because Jacob was in jail. He beat someone up in the emergency room. He didn't do any harm or anything. He was very, very, very upset because he needed help and no one would help him, so he started hitting someone on the head with a stick, I think it was. Maybe a nurse? I don't have all the facts. I don't blame him. No one likes to be ignored," she said and let this last phrase hang in the air, for my benefit.

"Okay," I said, "but you can't go around beating people up either."

"He's very depressed. He reminds me a lot of you, actually. I think he has seasonal affective disorder."

"It sounds to me like he has more than that."

"You might be right. How do I know? Last night they let him out of jail with no shoes? Why would they do that? Cliff and I try to do what we can for him."

I thought I remembered Cliff—a Marxist my mother's age who'd driven a city bus in San Francisco for many years. Also, one of the Go Bernies. Cliff was a functional friend.

"You're doing good work," I said. "Trying to help people who are worse off than yourself." This was AA talking. Not me. I was angry about the bathroom. AA had taught me not to express my feelings in situations like this where there was no point—I wasn't going to change her. Also, in situations like this I now found myself thinking of Nicola. I didn't quite understand how it worked, but I knew that the love I did feel for my mother (and possibly the fact that I felt any at all) was somehow sustained by Nicola, even though I had already decided not to tell Nicola about the bathroom.

"It's true, isn't it?" my mother said.

"What's true?" I asked.

"You really can't be responsible for another human being like Jacob, can you?"

"No," I said after a minute. "You can't."

*

Nicola and I started trying to get pregnant with the understanding that it might take quite some time. In less than two weeks, Nicola came out of the bathroom with her test and said, "I'm pregnant." We both lay back on the bed and held hands as we stared at the ceiling. I felt as if we were floating into the current of a river.

Our daughter was scheduled to be born in late fall. As the date approached, I spent long periods of time looking out the window. Most of the leaves had fallen. Those that remained were brown and closed, ready to fall. People walked in the woods next to our house bundled in down jackets and wool hats pulled over their brows. The winter light this far north was low on the horizon. In the mornings, a mist hung over the valley.

I still couldn't believe we owned a house that looked out at the woods. It had a fireplace in the living room where I sometimes liked to grade papers. When I sat in front of the fireplace, I didn't just feel content or at ease. I felt in control. Having grown up in a more stable home, Nicola didn't quite understand my need to feel in control of my life. When I gave into this need, I started to turn away from people, I started seeing my students as a burden, I stopped wanting to take risks in my writing or in life in general. I just wanted to be alone in front of the fire with my own thoughts where I was of no use to anyone, particularly myself. Still, I couldn't help it. I wanted to feel in control, and one thing I knew I couldn't control was the birth of our daughter. I knew everything was about to change, but I wanted to know what, exactly, this would look like. Some people with kids tried to explain it to me: *You'll have zero time, and you'll feel things you've never felt before.* I found it more helpful when parents just shook their heads and said, *You'll see.*

One of the mechanics working on our Subaru in Eugene came to pick me up because we only had one car and the garage was less than a mile down the hill from our house. He was a small guy, a little younger than me, with blond hair and large blue eyes. As we drove down the hill, we talked about the weather. His car smelled of grease. He had washed his hands, but the grease was rubbed into the cracks. We talked about the narrow, unsafe road leading up to our house, and he mentioned that he'd recently seen a mother and daughter riding up this road with the daughter on the back of the bike. He couldn't believe how scary it was. I told him I was about to have a daughter, and his whole body jumped in his seat.

"Man," he said, "I love my daughter! I'm so happy for you. I mean, really. It was the greatest thing that ever happened to me!"

So excited that I thought he might drive off the road, he told me how she went to the Spanish immersion school and how she was five now and could sing Christmas carols in Spanish.

"It's amazing, man! I mean, I love my daughter," he told me again as his eyes watered. When we reached the garage at the bottom of the hill, we kept talking as we stood in the parking lot. I told him I had no idea what I was doing, but I guessed I would figure things out as I went.

He touched my shoulder and looked me in the eyes. "It will open your heart," he said. "It will change you forever. Suddenly you realize that all these women walking around here—" he nodded across the street at the café where undergrads sat and studied, "they are a sister, a mother, a daughter. My advice," he said, "is listen to her. Listen to what she has to say. At the end of the day, that's what I look forward to. I want to hear everything she has to say."

*

Without quite realizing what was happening, I began to focus less on myself and my mother and more on this life that was about to join us. It was like watching a football travel from someone's hand and arc through the air. At first, she was just an idea traveling through space and time, her relationship to me mostly theoretical. Then she reached an apogee and spiraled downward toward my outstretched arms. I was no longer Jason Brown watching the football; I was Jason Brown who might drop the football. I didn't even like football, as a sport or as a metaphor. Now that I was about to be a father, it seemed as if I should know something about football.

On a screen in the doctor's office, a small kidney-bean smudge appeared. The bean seemed to be trying to escape, but the movement might have come from the technician moving the wand around.

"Look, baby foot!" the technician said.

I saw a flipper waving in the black space of the pod. Later, when we received the pictures by email from the center, there was a photo of the bean on which the technician, or someone, had written BABY FOOT!! in yellow caps. There were also two X marks connected by a dotted line that spanned the length of the 0.51-centimeter foot. Another photo contained the labels HEAD and LOWER BODY without exclamation marks.

At nineteen weeks we went in for Nicola's third ultrasound, this time at the office of the genetics counselor. We were told we were about to engage in a geriatric birth.

"Is that her elbow?" Nicola asked, squinting. She was tired. Had not been sleeping too well.

"That is baby's shoulder," the technician said and quickly zeroed in on the heart. An actual heart working away like the valves of a sports car.

"Holy shit, this is gonna really happen," Nicola said.

"There is baby's profile," the technician said in her sing-song voice.

There was a profile—a distinct jawline and nose and cheekbones. A spine curving down from the shoulder. An arm. She seemed to be sitting in the cockpit of a space capsule gripping the controls.

As we walked to the car, Nicola stopped and looked over her shoulder at the building.

"All they do in there all day long is show people ultrasounds of their babies. All day, every day."

I knew what she meant. I was stunned and floating because we had seen *our* baby. Not endless images of everyone else's babies.

Soon we received a glossy brochure in the mail. Nicola carried it to the kitchen table and opened it. *What is genetics counseling?*

"Yikes, why is someone asking us that?" I asked.

"We have to look at this," she said.

"Can't we not?"

What is a prenatal diagnosis? Birth defects? Who should consider reproductive genetics counseling and/or diagnosis? Women who have had a positive maternal serum screening test. Women who have had an abnormal finding on a previous ultrasound. Women/couples who have had a child with a chromosome abnormality such as Down's Syndrome or a birth defect such as spina bifida or a heart defect. Women/couples who have a family history . . .

We needed to make decisions about things like the Nuchal Translucency Ultrasound, the Detailed Anatomy, Level-2 Ultrasound or the Biochemical Screening, the Noninvasive Prenatal Testing (NIPT), the Inherited Genetic Carrier Screening, Chronic Villi Sampling (cvs), and Amniocentesis. Did these tests guarantee a Normal Baby? No. *What happens if an ABNORMALITY is found?* The woman/couple would be notified and given a full report of the findings, which would not include the things I actually feared our daughter might inherit from my mother's side of the family, i.e., mental illness and addiction. Things that might not show up for years to come. The goal was to aid the woman/couple by providing information. The philosophy and principles of the center: nonjudgmental and nondirective counseling. This meant that the woman/couple were not told what to do. The information was explained—sort of—to the woman/couple and the various options laid out (if there were any) so they could totally freak out on their own time and be relieved of the option of suing CGMFM for giving directive advice that seemed sound at the time, statistically speaking, but later resulted in death or something worse.

"Does everyone have to go through this?" I said.

"No, some people don't have medical insurance, or they live in places without modern medicine. They don't have to go through this."

*

One afternoon I headed out the back door of the building where I worked on campus with the dogs in tow. In the field behind the building, they tore after the ground squirrels. I closed my eyes and took a deep breath of the cool, Oregon air. When I opened my eyes, I saw the dogs returning to me. I hadn't called my mother back in more than a week even though she had left several messages.

According to campus code, people were supposed to keep their dogs leashed—a reasonable rule that most people followed. Not me. I liked feeling in control, but I did not like being told what to do. We crossed the courtyard of the education building and entered another field next to the library. Franny, our youngest, shot across the field like a bullet. Her legs kicked out, her ears slid back. She crossed the field in seconds and vanished into the tall trees of the Pioneer Graveyard.

In a matter of days, we would be in the hospital waiting for our daughter to appear. Watching Franny run flat out with her ears pulled back, I thought of Kierkegaard's phrase, "The soul remembers the beauty it used to know." In general, however, this was the kind of sentiment that one could only have about one's own dog. Other people did not always share my feelings. Skateboarders, bikers, runners—all of which abounded on campus—triggered her herding instinct and she sometimes went for their heels. I'd been yelled at and scolded many times, but for reasons I didn't fully understand (beyond a vague sense that the rules didn't apply to me), I'd refused to put her on a leash. Cheever and I followed her into the graveyard where I relaxed because there were fewer people. As soon as I stepped past the first row of headstones, I spotted a runner a hundred yards away. Franny was selective about herding runners. Some interested her, some did not. She was invariably attracted to jerks. She didn't see him right away, but she did stop and look at me. She and I tended to agree on who was a jerk and who wasn't. She looked where I was looking, and she took off after him.

I called for her to stop, more for the runner's benefit than anything else. I knew she wouldn't stop. About ten yards away from him, she got low and started her herding bark. He was over six feet, skinny, somewhere in his late fifties. I didn't recognize him, exactly, but I knew the type. He was, if not a dean, certainly some kind of associate dean or vice something in charge of fear and loathing. He was one of *them*. After many years of trying not to stereotype university administrators, I'd given up. It was an indulgence, like a five-dollar latte, that made me feel better in the moment. There was the officer corps, and there were the enlisted troops. In the modern university, most faculty were enlisted and noncoms. Us and them. Occasionally, one of us crossed over and within a matter of months started to look and act like them. The suit, the martial gait, the whole nine yards.

When Franny snapped at his ankle, he screeched like a bunny and leapt into the air. Her job done (the guy had stopped as surely as any sheep would have), Franny immediately sat on her haunches and took this opportunity to catch her breath. When she panted, it looked like she was smiling, which didn't help the situation. The guy did a little dance around her, as if he were being surrounded by piranhas, then tore out his Bluetooth earbuds.

"You, you, you!" He pointed at me. "That dog should be on a *leash.*"

I nodded in assent and called Franny over. She sat at my feet, and I slipped on her leash.

"This is against the *law*," the guy yelled and shook his fist at me. I wondered if he could tell that I was one of *them*, one of the faculty. "What is your name?"

Since my teenage years, it had been my policy in these situations to say as little as possible, especially regarding my identity. I half-heartedly uttered that I was sorry. His face boiled into a rage. I realized, not for the first time, that I'd been caught in an act of an utterly stupid rebellion against an amorphous authority. The rebel who had lost his cause. Even framed in an ironic context, I knew right away that the word *rebel* represented a side of myself that Rousseau had called "amour propre"—the narcissist starring in his own drama, imagining how he looks to an admiring audience.

I felt like calling my mother to tell her about the whole episode. I knew she would recognize the encounter from her own life and laugh. Humor always brought us together and relieved us both, if only temporarily, of the burden of self.

I looked at my phone as the runner stared at me, possibly waiting for a more sincere expression of my contrition, and I realized that my mother would not be there with us for the birth of her granddaughter. My mother would never be alone with my daughter. She couldn't be trusted, mentally or physically. I hadn't trusted my mother for a long time, probably since I could walk, but I was still waiting for the facts to change.

I felt tears in my eyes and on my cheeks, momentarily throwing the runner standing in front of me off his game, though he quickly recovered and fumed at me. He must have suspected that my tears were not for him. I sympathized with his frustration—I wanted to tell him that. When I saw my mother, I often felt the way he was feeling now.

"I'm about to have a baby," I said to the runner. He groaned and looked at me in the way you might look at a disturbed person on the street who asks if they can borrow your car. The kind of thing that happened in Eugene.

He took out his phone, dialed, and asked to speak to an officer. Then he described the middle-aged white male with two "collie dogs" standing in front of him. He described where he was and said that he'd been attacked—not quite attacked, but barked at.

"Okay," I said and headed off to the edge of campus at a light jog in my rubber L.L. Bean hunting boots. The dogs trotted along happily. The runner followed at pace ten feet behind. He'd been on hold after speaking to the dispatcher, I guessed, but now had reached an officer at the police station. He explained the situation all over again from the beginning and finished off with the update that the perpetrators—me and my dogs—were headed south toward the edge of the Pioneer Graveyard. "Now crossing Eighteenth Street," I heard as I crossed Eighteenth Street. "Headed west on Eighteenth Street." I looked over my shoulder, and there he was jogging on the balls of his feet with his phone pressed to his ear. I looked up but Eugene didn't have a police helicopter.

✳

When Nicola yelled from the bathroom with a towel between her legs at six a.m. on November 19, the TV show in my head began to roll. I had only experienced birth on TV shows and in movies. Even when things didn't work out in Netflix Originals, they did work out. People who died appeared in another show next year.

We had our "go bags," just as they did in the baby class video we'd watched where the actors pretending to be parents seemed so calm. I hurried everything to the car while Nicola called the doctor to confirm that we should go to the hospital. Because what if we shouldn't? How would the scene progress now that expectations had been raised and the physical uncertainties had been introduced onstage?

Around the time of my father's birth, my grandfather was fighting inland from D-Day beachhead. How had my grandmother handled that? D-Day, Battle of the Bulge, the bronze star. I didn't see how this drama, my drama, could compare. Why was it a competition?

Nicola snapped her fingers in my face and pointed to the dogs. "Front and center, please. Dogs! Your job." She headed to the car.

As I shut the dogs away downstairs with water and food (I called a friend to walk them) and carried Nicola's things to the car, I could only think in narrative clichés: I was *rushing headlong* toward *the most important moment of my life*. I felt almost exactly as I had during a trip to Afghanistan in 2014—my foray into journalism. I was a tourist. My *heart pounded* and my *thoughts raced*.

Arriving at the hospital was like arriving at a Marriott. Nicola said she wasn't in pain, but her eyes were wide, and her hair stood straight up in back. We had our luggage piled in front of the reception desk, where a young woman with dyed blonde hair asked how she could help us. Nicola seemed too stunned to speak, so I said, "We're having a baby." The woman nodded as if I'd asked for an extra pillow and produced some paperwork for us to fill out.

The phone rang—my mother—so I answered it. She said she wanted to meet us at the hospital. We shouldn't go through this experience "alone."

Either Nicola could hear the conversation, or she knew from the look on my face what conversation was taking place. She and I had already discussed this: my mother would not be coming to the hospital.

"We're not going through this alone," I said to my mother. "We're going through this together. Nicola and I together."

"But I really should be there," my mother said.

"I really think we need to do this on our own," I said and told her I had to go. Nicola took the phone from me and pressed the red button. It seemed wrong to hang up on my mother, but I knew it was necessary. Our daughter hadn't even been born yet, and I could feel the slow shift in my center of gravity.

I thought we might receive a keycard and just walk up to our room, but we needed an escort to the fifth-floor maternity center. When we got off the elevator, I expected to smell babies, though it occurred to me that I had no idea what babies smelled like. Not really. It smelled like a hospital—antiseptic under interrogation lights. The atmosphere of disaster. This was where people came to be told they would not be leaving. People in scrubs collecting a mortality tax. The smell was too chemical to be salt water, a smell engineered to communicate CLEAN in the same way Kentucky Fried Chicken emits a smell meant to communicate FOOD. A lie meant to kill you. People on other floors were dying. People choosing the opioid haze in their last hours, people choosing to gut it out so they could be "present," whatever that meant. We stood at some kind of reception area with no windows where a security guy asked me for my ID.

"Where are you?" Nicola asked. A familiar phrase designed to penetrate to some semi-authentic version of "me" buried beneath layers of *me*. I was now learning that I had to prove who I was and receive a bracelet that would allow me to enter the maternity center. This was necessary, the security guy told us, to make sure no one ran off with someone else's baby.

"People steal other people's babies?" I said incredulously. He nodded.

We followed a nurse into the inner sanctum where babies came into being. I wanted to feel that there was something sacred about such a place and the people who worked here. But the nurses looked exhausted and depressed, maybe because of the buzzing fluorescent lights, the CLEAN! smell, or the gray industrial carpet with the foot traffic patch no industrial cleaner would ever remove. The carpet reminded me of the entrance to my mother's apartment building. I pictured stolen babies being dragged down the carpet toward the exit to be sold on the Dark Web.

Aside from the hard tile floor and the medical bed the size of a throne, our room was about as nice as you might expect from a Marriott. I'd only stayed in a Marriott a few times; we stayed in La Quintas on the road. There was a window seat overlooking a deep green field and wooded hills beyond. A nice place to spend the weekend. Nicola sat in an easy chair and set her bag on the floor.

"Now what?" she said.

A doctor showed up, a bit of a sloven, reminding me of me. "How's it going?" he asked Nicola.

"Okay," she said from her easy chair.

"That kinda worries me. Your water has broken and you're okay. I'm gonna give you Oxytocin to hurry things along. Nothing to worry about. No sweat. Just to make sure we're making progress."

"We're not making progress?" Nicola said.

"We're not *not* making progress, but we'd like to see a little more progress."

His face was wrinkled but his teeth were great, and he smiled as if he was handing us a lottery check. I had a bias toward good-teeth people. They seemed less likely to fuck up.

"Something we should worry about?" I said.

"Not," he said, "to worry at all. I'll be back shortly."

But he wasn't. A nurse arrived with the Oxytocin, and she talked reassuringly about all that we'd go through. I would coach Nicola along per the video I'd watched at parent training. The breathing and encouragement. There might be some "options" along the way (options?), decision points, you know, but nothing major, and Nicola was so healthy things would sail right along. Saying she would be back to discuss the epidural, the nurse sailed out of the room.

"Options?" Nicola said, ten minutes too late.

Nicola had resisted the idea of the epidural but she had just taken Oxytocin—to move things along—so what did it matter now? The drug-free idealism was out the window. We'd talked about the importance, in theory, of being present for such a *beautiful and life-changing experience* (as one brochure described it), but I could see now that she was just scared.

"If it's between me and the baby, it's the baby," Nicola mumbled, and I said I didn't think that this was what the nurse had meant by "options."

"That's why we're here," I said and waved my hand at the room, the hospital, America (our version of America). We were no longer worried about what might be "unnatural" or about the absurd advantages of this medical Marriott swarming with doctors, nurses, and machines. We would sacrifice any ideal (not that we had many) to give *our* child a better chance. This was not a flattering impulse to recognize. This was foxhole thinking, which might be the only honest kind.

Another nurse arrived to replace the previous nurse who'd gone home, as nurses do when their shifts are over. "I'm Blah Blah," she said. I couldn't hear her name, and she asked how Nicola was doing.

"I don't know what I am," she said. "I think I want it to be over. Why isn't it over?"

We heard a low moan from the far wall that presumably separated our room from another, identical room in the medical Marriott.

"Do you think the dogs are okay?" Nicola asked.

The moaning turned to screaming and grew so loud that the woman next door could've been in the same room. No fictionalized Netflix version of CIA torture had ever sounded so terrifying. Nicola shook her head grimly. The screaming subsided for a moment, and I thought: that was awful but it's over. Now there's a baby. But the screaming returned a few seconds later with twice the force.

Our nurse appeared standing next to a different doctor.

"So, your water broke?" the doctor said. He measured the dilation of her cervix. We were shooting for a ten but were only at a six. "That's okay, no problem," he said and announced that they were upping her dosage. Then he vanished. The screaming from next door stopped. Either someone next door had been born or everyone had died.

"Do you hear that humming sound?" Nicola said.

"That's the building, I think."

The sun went down. We weren't awake, but we weren't asleep. They had measured the dilation of Nicola's cervix three times now, and she'd progressed but not enough. We had a new nurse, an older woman who'd had a couple of kids, she told us, and had a lot to say about living in Georgia.

Nicola was no longer doing fine. She was in pain, and it was the middle of the night. She squeezed her eyes shut, clenched my hand, bared her teeth, and nodded slightly. The nurse and anesthesiologist inserted a tube into Nicola's lower back. With wavy black hair and a permanent smile, the anesthesiologist reminded me of an actor playing a doctor on TV. After delivering his bolus, he breezed out of the room with a wave. In moments, Nicola's eyes glazed, and she relaxed.

The polysyllabic drug names and their cause and effect relationship to the anatomy of this person, Nicola, who I didn't think I could live without, combined with the constant smiling on the part of the nurses, my lack of sleep, the strange humming sound coming either from the building or my head, the periodic squeaking of rubber soles on the mirror-polished floors outside our room, not to mention the nurse's endless chipper conversation about the general wonderfulness of babies and the *life-changing experience* we were apparently undergoing—I entertained the sleep-deprived delusion that the nurse might be a robot or, even worse, a person only 23 percent present and 77 percent elsewhere.

Also, on closer inspection, the furnishings of our birthing room were not quite authentic (the wood grain of the paneling and the sides of the window seat, for instance, repeated in a precise pattern that would never happen in nature, and the seat coverings were either not-cotton or not-wool and might even be, like the not-wood furniture, a kind of nonporous *plastic* that could be sanitized should there be a problem with bodily fluids), all of it communicating that everything was *fine* and that no deviation from the plan was necessary (or possible). In reality it felt like everything was falling apart.

Nicola's eyes shot open in her pale moon face. It was as if a fist inside her head twisted her features, and before she could even speak, I knew she was in more pain than could be described.

I called the nurse over and pointed to Nicola. "Well, oh dear," the nurse said, "you seem to be in some discomfort." Nicola groaned and tried to nod. It was like watching someone have a conversation while they were being struck by lightning. Another nurse arrived. "Some discomfort, I see." They called for the anesthesiologist to return. Maybe the insertion of the needle had been unsuccessful, or maybe it had come loose. The anesthesiologist strolled in—from the beach, it seemed—and they turned Nicola on her side to check the insertion point. Then they checked the tubes traveling up to the machine that was supposed to pump the painkiller down into the spinal cord and erase the unpleasant aspect of what was happening here. The machine had small plastic or glass orbs that you might expect to light up and indicate all was well and functioning, only they were dark.

"Are those lights supposed to be on?" I asked. The two nurses and the anesthesiologist all looked at the machine. Then one of the nurses reached up and flipped a switch. The lights turned on.

So, apparently good teeth offered no guarantee of competence.

*

A new doctor explained that it was time to discuss our "options"— that dreaded word. After a minute, she stopped talking to Nicola and faced me. Nicola was too out of it. Her water had broken so long ago, and the baby seemed stuck, essentially. Either the baby was too big or the pelvis was slightly tilted or both. We'd arrived at a point where there was a "danger to the baby" if we prolonged the process. We needed to talk about the possibility of a C-section.

I'd heard the word "danger" in relation to Nicola and the baby— the word I'd suspected I would hear all along—but it had been spoken with the tone of someone discussing the weather. Since we'd resolved the on/off switch problem of the painkiller machine, we'd been sitting in this birthing room listening to the hum of institutional indifference while the nurse had walked into our room, checked various readings, checked the dilation progress, etc., all with the same smile, and there'd been no mention of "danger to the baby." Now, quite casually, almost as an off-hand comment, there was a possibility of *Danger to the Baby*.

"You need to make a decision."

We were not in a TV show, and I was not an actor. The doctor nodded at me. Clearly, I was supposed to make a decision in real life.

"Is there a decision to make?" I asked. Why were we having this discussion?

I announced that I thought we would go ahead with the C-section because the alternative seemed to be death. I looked at Nicola to see if she understood. She nodded, though I wasn't sure what she understood.

Another doctor arrived—the OBGYN from Eugene who both Nicola and I trusted for some reason. She announced that we'd be moving to surgery, but not right away. There was a queue. Even though the word "danger" had been used, we were in a line, not that different from a line at Starbucks, except in this case waiting could kill a child. That was my understanding.

The OBGYN started talking about a different danger, something to do with the anesthesia they would administer for the C-Section, which might cause a problem—"pose a slight *danger*"—to the child in that moment before she was "removed." I wanted to know what kind of danger. A "slight," just a slight (*a small degree, a person of insufficient build or, as a verb, an insult*) chance, relative, say, to proceeding "naturally," which was not recommended, that there would be "*danger* to the baby." I had more questions, but everyone left in a hurry before I could speak. Nicola and I were alone. She tried to speak but only mumbled with her eyes half open. I couldn't put my finger on exactly what'd gone wrong, but I was certain that the lives of the most important people in my life were being endangered because people we didn't know were letting it happen.

Or maybe everything was okay, and no one was bothering to tell me it was okay because what was happening was utterly ordinary for them and extraordinary only for us because it was happening to us. They were just pedestrians in our lives. We would never see any of these health-care professionals again unless we all happened to be shopping at Market of Choice on the same afternoon.

"What's happening?" Nicola finally said.

"Everything is fine," I said, "don't worry." I told her people were coming back, any second now, and then we were going to do a C-section. She nodded with her eyes closed. I had the impulse to order a pizza. What I really wanted was a handful of Percocet. Finally, they came for Nicola and wheeled her away. Maybe the whole thing would happen without me. I needed to be with her to make sure nothing went wrong. I was given blue scrubs and a funny mesh hat and put in a bathroom near the surgery and told to stay put. I was happy that I'd not yelled at anyone or started crying.

The door opened, and a nurse, taking me by the arm, led me like a dog down the hall to the OR where I saw Nicola, or the upper half of Nicola, lying on her back. Her lower half was screened off. Several people leaned over her stomach, which I thankfully couldn't see. Nicola was awake, looking at me with astonishment. Her lower half, I'd been told, was numb. Bright lights, hushed talk. A secret cabal, I thought, stirring the pot in *Macbeth*. Why was I the only man in the room? An interloper. I didn't belong here. The nurse who'd brought me in stood by my side. I realized her sole duty was to babysit me. My handler. She repositioned me slightly. I'd been standing in the path the baby would take when she was "removed" from Nicola. I distinctly heard, "Okay, put the uterus back in. . . ."

Two of the nurses attending to Nicola behind the blue sheet suddenly raced away from her. One of them carried a creature. As they passed me without a word and entered the adjacent room, I turned to watch them go and felt a metallic creak deep in my chest, like a rusty bolt yielding under the pressure of a wrench.

My handler steered me through the door into the room where I stood with three nurses around a small table that held our daughter. Her eyes were closed. She was gray, and she wasn't breathing. They couldn't get her to breathe. The nurses' hands darted around the baby (I couldn't bear to even think her name, *Isabella*, not until she breathed, and she had yet to *breathe*). Someone slipped a mask onto her small mouth. Someone else took her vitals and oxygen levels. They spoke code to each other in a clipped, even tone. One nurse squeezed a bulb to pump air into her lungs. Her tiny ribs expanded like a paper bag being inflated. The other nurse repositioned her lifeless limbs, which flopped like strands of rubber. The anesthesia that had wormed its way through Nicola had suffocated our daughter before she'd even taken her first breath.

The nurse stopped squeezing the bulb, removed the mask from the baby's face, and we all waited. Her chest rose like the forehead of a porpoise breaking the ocean surface. Her blue eyes snapped open, her limbs jolted, and the air filled with Isabella's cry.

Animal Stories

"What you have to understand," my mother said when we parked and headed into the Sweet Life bakery for her birthday, which occurs on December 31, every year, "is that I've had a lot to deal with lately with Boots." My mother had been doing quite well since Bella's birth. Either this was one of her periodic upswings, or it was part of a positive trend. I was, as always, susceptible to believing in the latter. The apartment manager was performing monthly inspections of her place as a condition of continued habitation. She spent time with her friends, the Go Bernies, with whom she attended rallies and outdoor movies. They protested with signs on the side of the road. My mother had been to our house several times to play with Bella. She was nice to Nicola.

Bella had squirmed in Nicola's lap when we first sat down for dessert, but now she was pacified staring at my mother. Over the years, my mother had grown slightly wild-eyed, and she tended to roll her head while she talked. I watched Bella watching my mother. I'd become the kind of middle-aged fool I would have laughed at as a teenager—gazing at his family, always smiling. I was the scourge of hard-boiled adolescents everywhere. Bella seemed to change a bit every time I turned around. All she had to do was look at me and blink and I felt like I was going to fall over. The knowledge that what I felt had been felt by countless other fathers and parents stretching back through time did not lessen the power of what I was experiencing. In bringing Bella into the world, Nicola and I had crossed a threshold and started to give ourselves over to life in a way that I still didn't understand.

"Who's Boots?" Nicola asked after we had ordered our slices of pie. Though Nicola had weathered a number of skirmishes with my mother, Bella's birth had softened her defenses. She seemed to be interested in my mother's response. My mother had recently declared that Nicola was okay both because she was the kind of person who could appreciate a good story and because she had proven herself to be an animal person. "In fact," my mother had said, "she's a better animal person than me." My mother's highest compliment for anyone.

Boots was a cat belonging to a woman who lived two doors down from my mother. I'd only met Boots a few times, in passing, but I was fully acquainted with his story. He was one of the wayward cats in the neighborhood my mother tracked. The last time I'd seen him, he was limping, missing patches of fur, and only opened one eye. The lid over what may have been an empty socket (I didn't want to know) remained closed. Before my mother started to tell us her tale, I knew that Boots's trajectory had to have taken a sharp turn for the worse. There was only one way for things to go in most stories. Nicola sensed this as well and shot me a grimace.

The woman who took care of Boots (Stacey, Boots's "owner" in air quotes, because Boots was feral and refused to sleep inside) had become my mother's nemesis. The woman had "pretended to care" for Boots for many years—she put out food and kept a cardboard box under the eaves of her front porch for Boots to sleep in during the cold season.

Given the substandard level of cat care, my mother told us that we would not be surprised that Boots had disappeared. "Gone. No trace." My mother had started taking long walks with Tillie, who wasn't friends with Boots, though they tolerated each other. My mother, whistling in the bushes along the river, called for Boots over and over. Sometimes she carried a piece of chicken and waved it around.

"I met some interesting people down there," my mother said.

"I bet," Nicola said.

My mother had gathered a small search party, some of them tent residents of the riverbank, and they whistled for Boots in the park. "No Boots," my mother said. Then one day my mother noticed that Stacey had taken Boots's cardboard box inside and there was no bowl. My mother banged on her door and asked what had happened to

Boots's house and food. It was the middle of winter. "I have my own cats to worry about!" Stacey yelled at my mother and accused her of trying to make her look bad in front of the whole community. "You do look bad!" my mother yelled back.

The next day my mother spotted Boots in the bushes near Stacey's apartment. My mother tried to call Boots over, but Boots fled. He wanted nothing to do with people. "You can't blame him," my mother said. "The human race sucks."

The pie and cake we'd ordered arrived, but my mother would not be interrupted. A week went by in the story about Boots, and once again he had disappeared. In that time more people from the neighborhood joined the search. No Boots. Then just the other day my mother was driving home when she saw him splayed out on the side of the road. She left her car (still registered under my name) in the middle of the road with the engine running and the door open and ran to Boots's side. He was still *breathing*. She carried Boots into the park—the park, if you thought about it, she said, should be called "Boots Park"—and sat by the river where he liked to hunt birds and other critters.

"Where's the car during all this?" I interrupted her.

"I don't know," she said.

In any case, Boots looked up at my mother and gazed into her eyes with his one good eye. "It's okay, Boots," she said, or something like that, she couldn't quite remember. His breathing grew shallow, his eye dimmed.

"And then he was dead," my mother said.

Bella stared at my mother with her mouth open and eyes wide.

"He died right there?" Nicola asked. She hadn't eaten any of her pie.

"Well, I could still feel his heart beating very faintly, but his eye was empty and staring out. He was on his way. Then Boots and I sat by the river for a while just listening to the sound of the water. Can you imagine what it's been like to go through all this?" my mother asked.

"Yes," I said.

"Do you know how old I am today?" my mother asked.

"Seventy-five," I said.

"That's right." She seemed surprised.

"Happy New Year," I said.

*

Not long after the tale of Boots was told, my mother called and said that Tillie wouldn't eat or drink water and had lost at least 20 percent of her weight in just a few days. I said the obvious—the cat needed to go to the vet. At the vet, an X-ray revealed that she had tumors throughout her whole body. They suggested that my mother put the cat down right away unless she was prepared to embark on very expensive cancer treatment at the vet school in Corvallis. I wished they hadn't held this out as an option.

"What do you think?" my mother asked. I said I didn't know that "we" could really spend that kind of money and immediately regretted how I'd framed the situation. "We" was not a good way to start any financial discussion. Her Social Security funneled directly to her basic living expenses. "We" meant me, and for various reasons having to do with my modest public university salary, Nicola staying at home to take care of the baby, and my profligate Starbucks habit, "we" were not going to spend thousands of dollars trying to save a cat that the vet said probably couldn't be saved for any amount of money. The phrase *she's just a cat* passed through my mind but fortunately didn't make its way to my mouth. She was my mother's cat—that was the point, of course. My mother was my mother, I was her son, and Tillie was her cat.

I acknowledged that Tillie was "part of the family" on the same level as our two dogs and even, my mother implied by mentioning Isabella's name, our human child, but I asked my mother to consider the suffering that Tillie would have to endure for even a chance of survival. I also asked her what odds the vet had given Tillie under the best of circumstances? She said that was a good question.

"Why don't *we* start there?" I said, and my mother hung up to call the vet. Of course, the vet couldn't talk right away, and when my mother called me back later that afternoon, I was too busy and didn't pick up. I didn't feel good about this strategy. The one I was familiar with. When my mother and I spoke the next morning, she reported that the vet could not give specific odds. My mother would have to see the specialist for that kind of information. The vet was willing to offer "not good" as a general prognosis and reminded my mother that the cat might be suffering, which I took to mean that Tillie was definitely experiencing unbearable pain.

"She doesn't seem to be suffering," my mother said.

"Ahh, that's the thing about cats," I said gently. "They don't speak English. And they are Stoics."

"We need to keep her away from Trump," my mother said.

"But seriously, from what you say, Tillie doesn't eat, doesn't drink, doesn't move around, just stares at the wall. That sounds like pain to me."

"She'll drink if I pour water down her throat."

"I don't think that counts. In any case, I don't think anyone deserves to suffer that much."

"No one deserves to suffer," my mother agreed, though she stopped short of agreeing that Tillie was "ready to go."

Satisfied that I had at least steered the ship off the path of operations and chemotherapy, I told my mother that when the time was right, we would have a nice ceremony of some kind.

"Yes, somewhere on family land."

"Family land? You mean spreading the ashes at our house?" By "our" house I meant the house belonging to Nicola and me, but I knew my mother had heard that differently.

Nicola had been sitting across from me at our kitchen table during my conversation with my mother. She now looked up from her computer and narrowed her eyes at me.

"Ashes, no," my mother said. "I'm not going to hand her over to the ovens."

"I don't think that's a comparison you want to make."

"I'm not making a comparison. I'm talking about a member of the family here," she said.

"I know, I know." I agreed that when the time came, we would bury Tillie in our backyard and that I would make a coffin of solid wood—not composite or plywood—and a grave marker of some kind and that there would be an actual ceremony.

"In our backyard?" Nicola said when I hung up. I knew what she meant. We lived on a steep slope. "Most of that hill is clay and sandstone. And animals come through from the park."

I told Nicola not to worry. My mother's old dog Piper and a previous cat were dying for more than a year before she was willing to let them go. We probably wouldn't have to deal with the problem right away.

Two days later my mother called and said her cat was dead.

I said what I always said: "How are you doing?"

"How can you ask that question? It's been a horror show over here." Tillie had continued to refuse to eat or drink or move around, so my mother carried her outside and around the block on their usual walk. At some point she took in a little water, but soon she started coughing. Small cat coughs at first, then a horrible rasping. She began to cough up blood and emit a low, plaintive, continuous moan that kept them both up all night.

"Why didn't you take her to the vet?"

"Well, it was the weekend, and the vet was closed. I could have gone to the emergency vet, but they are expensive, and I know how you hate *expensive*."

"It would've been worth the money!" I said and groaned at the idea of the creature's suffering. "For God's sake."

"She started this strange gurgling?"

"The death rattle," I said.

"Finally, she settled down enough for me to read her a poem."

I was momentarily curious about what poem she had read.

"'The Idea of Order at Key West,'" she reported.

"You're kidding me."

"I would not kid in a situation like this. It's from some book you gave me. After the poem, she was at peace, and when I reached down, she was cold."

I found a few old pine boards in the rafters of the garage, cleared the cardboard boxes off the table saw, and cut the boards for a small coffin, twenty inches long by ten inches wide. Plenty of room for a cat, it seemed to me. I should've used cedar, which would've lasted longer, but I didn't have any cedar. I only had pine, or what Home Depot called "white board," which was not a species. Whatever was cheap they sold as "white board." I used brass screws to attach the boards. At least they wouldn't rust out.

I carried the box, the screw gun, a pocketful of screws, and a pick and shovel into the backyard. Like many houses in the northwest, ours was built on a slope, but there was a small flat area right below the house before the ground dropped off to the bottom of the property. Nicola, standing high above on the back deck, held Bella. Both of them peered over the railing as I hacked away at the clay and sandstone. Our back deck cantilevered out from our top floor, where one entered the house from the street side. Our living room and kitchen were on the top floor, our bedrooms on the floor below. From where I stood partway down the slope, the house seemed enormous, but in fact it was only thirteen hundred square feet with two small bedrooms. The perfect size for us. Our two Australian shepherds stood at Nicola's feet.

At first, I thought I would dig down to at least three feet—deep enough, maybe, to keep out the raccoons, nutrias, coyotes, and possums that wandered out of the nearby park. After twelve inches I hit sandstone and sat, totally exhausted. Nicola yelled down, and my mother appeared on the porch carrying a shoebox. Nicola looked concerned, the baby and the dogs looked intensely curious, and my mother looked as sad as I'd ever seen her. Bella raised her plump hand and waved it back and forth. I credited Bella for bringing us all together. Not just a new life but a new start and a higher purpose— the future. Bella, Nicola, my mother, my students, people I worked with in AA, the dogs—the circle of those I felt connected to and committed to. I wanted my mother to move to the inside of this circle and to be part of our future.

ANIMAL STORIES

"I think you better come up here," Nicola said. I climbed up the bank and the partially washed away stone steps along the side of the house to the street level, where I kicked off my boots and entered the house. My mother, standing in our small dining room, looked down at the box in her arms. Bella, who was growing at twice the rate of other babies, so it seemed to us, rested in Nicola's arms and furrowed her brow. The two dogs wiggled at the sight of my mother, though they held back from jumping on her as they usually did. They eyed her intensely. Whenever Nicola and I turned our backs, my mother pulled salty human snacks out of her pockets and fed them.

"Oh, Jason," she said and shook her head. She was already crying. I tried to hug her even though any physical contact with my mother caused an explosion in my head followed by a psychic numbness that spread like Novocain through my system.

"I know," I said and grabbed the box from her. She took my arm, and we walked out the door and along the path in front of the house. We descended the uneven steps along the side of the house slowly, a couple inches at a time. Twenty minutes later we reached the small hole I'd dug in the ground. I placed the shoebox inside the wooden coffin and placed the coffin in the hole. Of course, the hole was not deep enough; the box rose above ground level. I had to grab the shovel and dig deeper.

"That's okay," my mother said.

"It's not okay." I didn't want to explain why. Nicola, the baby, our two dogs and I—we were not the only animals out here.

When I'd dug out enough and covered the box with dirt, I took a folded piece of paper out of my pocket and asked my mother if she had anything she wanted to say. If not, I had part of Whitman's "Song of Myself." She shook her head with her eyes closed.

I think I could turn and live with animals,
They are so placid and self-contain'd,
I stand and look at them long and long.

They do not sweat and whine about their condition,
They do not lie awake in the dark and weep for their sins,
They do not make me sick discussing their duty to God,
Not one is dissatisfied, not one is demented with the mania
    of owning things,
Not one kneels to another, nor to his kind that lived thousands
    of years ago,
Not one is respectable or unhappy over the whole earth.

So they show their relations to me and I accept them,
They bring me tokens of myself. . . .

My mother thanked me and covered her face.

"Now what?" she said. "What am I supposed to do now?"

I looked up. There was Nicola's brown hair above Bella's perfectly round head and two dog snouts poking through the railing.

"Let's go up to the house," I said, "and we can all sit on the porch."

"Okay," she said and took my arm. "That would be nice."

As we climbed the moss-covered steps around the side of the house, she almost slipped several times. I had to steady her while she rested. In my mind, she was still forty years old and probably always would be. At the front door, she straightened up and took a deep breath.

"This is where you live," she said, as if she'd never been here before. She smiled and squeezed my arm. "This is your home."

✳

Nicola and I planned to spend several months living in a cabin in Colorado owned by Nicola's mother. I had a sabbatical from teaching, and Nicola wanted to rethink her work life (a former English major and aspiring poet, she did marketing for an architecture firm) and spend time raising our daughter.

When Nicola had brought me here shortly after we met, I'd fallen in love with the place and with her. To reach the cabin we had to drive along the twisting two-lane road that followed the river at the bottom of the canyon north of a scruffy old ranching community with sofas and rusty trucks in the front yards. The red canyon walls rose on either side of us. Tectonic plates had slipped under the surface of the continent eighty million years ago and pushed up to form these mountains. If the land was still slowly rising, it was also slowly falling as the wind and ice eroded the peaks into the valleys. The remains of prehistoric crocodiles were lodged in the striated rock in the jagged landscape undisturbed by the scars of human presence except for the contrails tracing the sky above. I tried to imagine the planet before there were so many people living on it, before the culture in which I had been raised, the culture that had metastasized over the globe, had forged the myth that man should dominate nature.

We turned off the pavement onto a narrow dirt road and started the climb to the top of the mesa and the cabin. Little if any work had been done on the place for more than twenty years. The wood siding was brittle and perforated by the wind and sun. I could break it off between my fingers. The wind poured in around the window frames, the bent metal chimney had never been cleaned, and the well water coughed out of the faucet in orange spatter. In a high wind the tin roof flapped because the screws had never been tightened. During storms the whole place shook as if from an earthquake. Probably in part because the place needed saving, I loved it. If I didn't get to work right away, we would never survive the winter. We had to secure the roof, cut firewood, get a sled so we could hike groceries in from the main road.

We were miles from a ski area. Because Nicola's mother had bought this place years ago, our family now had the opportunity to spend time immersed in the natural world. The absence of people was a relief. Except for the boundary lines on the county property website, life on the mesa was governed by laws that preceded human dominion.

To be in a place where human presence was tolerated provisionally and to sit in the dry grass as Bella learned to run across the field chasing our dogs filled me with a sense of vertigo. I wanted to stay here forever watching Bella wheel away from me on her springy two-year-old legs only to stop and turn around to make sure I was still there. "Papa," she would say, her voice cutting through the constantly blowing wind. Our Australian shepherds had a similar radar. They would race through the grass until they were twenty or thirty yards away, then arc toward us to touch base before racing away again. Nicola, Bella, the dogs, and I, we never tired of this ancient ritual of pulling away and circling back, of periodic contact: Bella's hand against my arm before she ran into the field again, a wet nose grazing my palm or rising to brush my cheek before following a scent into the scrub oak.

Except for a few roads and other cabins, we lived in the wilderness on the mesa. I had to keep an eye on Bella at all times. Several years before, my mother-in-law, getting ready to leave the cabin, placed her hand on the handle of the glass front door, but realized she'd forgotten her coffee mug and walked back through the kitchen. When she returned to the door, she found a mountain lion sitting on its haunches on the other side of the glass. Two years before, while on a visit from Eugene, I was walking our two dogs and my mother-in-law's lab a hundred yards south of the cabin when we came around a scrub oak to face a bear cub. The lab chased the cub into the bushes to our left. The mother bear appeared ten yards to our right and rose onto her hind legs. Franny, a little more than a year old, started barking. I grabbed her, turned in place, and ran west through the scrub—exactly what you're not supposed to do, I was later told. Cheever led the way as the branches scraped against my face and arms. I heard crashing behind me and kept running until I tripped on a stump and flew headfirst into the grass. There was nothing behind us except the twisted oaks and the sky.

It worried me that I could so easily shut out the rest of the world, and that I didn't seem to miss other people at all. If people could see themselves through the eyes of animals, I imagined that we would seem like a species of addicts exclusively focused on our insatiable desires. No amount of food, security, cars, plastic, money, alcohol, drugs, sex, or domination would ever fully anesthetize us. Nothing would ever be enough. If other creatures could ask one thing of us, I felt they would ask us to raise nonaddicted children. I worried that I didn't know how to do this and hoped that Nicola would have better ideas than I did. I also worried that I'd never be able to say no to Bella and that I would end up being a burden to her because my love for her was a feeling I couldn't live without. It wasn't love, I knew, if what I needed from her was more important than what she needed from me. She brought me so much joy and I loved her so much that I often felt overwhelmed, but it wasn't her job to fill my life with purpose. I was determined to put what she needed first, but I knew from experience that no one is more blind than the person who thinks they know what they are doing. To raise Bella, Nicola and I would have to rely on each other, and we would need other members of our family, including my mother, and we would need schools, neighbors, other kids, and parents. We would need help from a human world that we didn't fully trust.

*

While we were in Colorado, we rented our house in Eugene to a former student. My mother stayed in her apartment downtown in Eugene. Three things happened at more or less the same time—our tenant moved out earlier than we thought he would, my mother's landlord wanted her out (her lease had expired), and the world was beset by a global pandemic. We could have pushed to keep my mother in her apartment even though COVID eviction restrictions had yet to be enacted, but even if the landlord had agreed, he was going to raise the rent as much as he could. My sister and I talked about ways to placate the landlord, who had already exercised enormous patience with my mother at his own expense. She had damaged the apartment enough that we didn't think he would have trouble evicting her and coming after me for the damage. My sister and I paid my mother's rent, and we couldn't go any higher. The rents in Eugene had risen steadily over the last five years. Soon my sister and I would be paying rent that was equal to the mortgage Nicola and I paid for our house. Nicola wasn't working, we couldn't afford part-time day care. My sister and her husband earned good money, but they had a son and they lived in Brooklyn.

My mother had been happier for more than a year before our departure for Colorado. She had been huddling with the "Go Bernie" people and attending protests and city hall meetings to try to take down the system. She seemed to have some community. My sister talked to her frequently on the phone, while Bella and I visited with her regularly, usually at the dog park. Then we left for Colorado and COVID-19 hit; since that time she had started to complain constantly of isolation and loneliness.

Bella's birth had fostered a new and inflated sense of optimism and faith in my ability to overcome even the most trenchant problems, but when I called my mother to see what she thought of living in our house until we returned, at which point I would build her an apartment in our oversized garage, she was silent.

"What if I don't want to live up there with all those fancy people?"

"There are no fancy people," I said. "It's Eugene." After half an hour of persuading her that our neighborhood was not a right-wing stronghold, she grew lukewarm to the idea and finished off the conversation with, "I don't know, we'll see."

When I suggested to Nicola that my mother move into our house for the rest of my sabbatical and into a garage apartment thereafter, she studied me as if I had just returned from a long and perilous journey to the moon.

"Are you crazy?" she eventually said. Bella looked up at me as if she also expected me to answer this question.

I had to wait until after Bella fell asleep to pitch my idea a second time. I had formed a kind of presentation with clear points: we would save money on paying my mother's rent, we could use the savings for childcare, maybe my mother could provide some "supervised" childcare, the "apartment" I built in the garage would add to the value of our house. . . .

"And as an added bonus, every time I leave the house with Bella, I will run into your mom sitting in a lawn chair outside our garage ready to yell at me because you haven't met her needs," Nicola said. "What we've been doing—having her live across town—works because she is not right next to us."

"I will build a separate entrance on the other side of the garage. She won't be able to get in through the gate to our front door."

"A gate? Your mother is a criminal mastermind. You were the one who told me she failed the criminal test in Arizona."

"She did."

"Within a week, she would be living in the house, and we would be living in the garage."

"That seems extreme."

"Does it? When are you going to build this apartment in the garage with new windows, doors, floors, a bathroom and kitchenette? After work while your mother looks after Bella?"

"Sure," I said.

Nicola studied my face.

"You really want to try this, don't you?" she said.

I said I did. My friend Keith's mother had just died, and she hadn't been much older than my own mother. This seemed like the last opportunity to try. Of course, I had already run this idea by Keith, and he had told me, in no uncertain terms, that I was out of my mind.

"Okay," Nicola said, "go ahead and try."

Bella came into the room with all three of her stuffed unicorns somehow loaded in her arms—Papa Woodrow (the size of a German shepherd), which I had bought on sale at Lowe's, Mama Woodrow (about the size of a corgi), and Baby Woodrow (the size of a kitten). She kept repeating the phrase "Baby Woodrow booboo" because Baby Woodrow's horn was coming off. She was looking at me with her huge blue eyes because I was the one who knew how to sew.

I planned to drive back to Eugene in the middle of the pandemic and move my mother into our house. Then we could build an apartment attached to the garage that had a separate entrance, so we could all have good boundaries. On paper, it all seemed to make sense—to me, anyway. No one outside the closed loop of my own brain was cheering me on.

My mother had more than a month's warning that I was returning. For some reason, I assumed that she was spending this time preparing to move. On the phone she complained that it was hard to find boxes, so I talked her through a plan to pick up boxes. She complained that she had no packing tape, and I explained that there were places called stores that sold packing tape. Not just packing tape specific stores, I told her, but really almost any place that called itself a store sold tape.

"Are you writing this down?" she asked. "The way you speak to me? For *your* book."

"I thought it was *our* book. That's what you said."

"Not right now it's not. You would love it if people thought I was some kind of monster. A *ghoul*. That would suit your purposes."

"My purposes?"

"If I move into your place, who pockets the money? You didn't think I would catch that, did you?"

"Pocket the money?" I had formed a habit, which served no purpose, of lobbing her phrases back to her.

"I'm moving to Hawaii. What do you think about that? I bet that blows a hole in your plans to get rich off me. What're you gonna do now, big shot?"

I decided to hang up and call back fifteen minutes later. Sometimes that worked the way it did with restarting my computer to get rid of a glitch. When she answered, she said, "Yesssss," and I mentioned that the previous conversation hadn't gone very well. She agreed and asked if I was in a better mood now. I asked her if she didn't want to move into our house?

"What choice do I have? When Stalin commands, you do what Stalin says!"

I tried to explain in my strained calm voice that she did have a choice, of course, but when I thought about it, I wasn't so sure how much of this was true. Her landlord wanted her out so he could repair the damage she had caused to the apartment. We could fight him under the new COVID regulations, but that was a temporary solution and a bad idea. I would be lucky if he didn't come after me for thousands of dollars. She didn't have a social worker because she refused to work with one, she wasn't on a list for public housing because that was beneath her. She was dependent on me, and she hated to be dependent. She hated to be a burden.

"You just move me around like a piece of luggage," she said.

"I don't think that's really fair," I said.

"Fair . . . hah, hah, hah. You hear that?"

"Do you think this is fun, trying to deal with this?"

"Someone's having fun, and it's not me."

I told her if she didn't want to live in our house or the apartment in the garage . . .

"What apartment?" she said. "There *is* no apartment in your garage!"

"But there *will be*," I said with enough emphasis, it seemed to me, to convince anyone that the apartment was a fait accompli.

"Can you describe for me what this apartment will look like?" she said.

"Large and comfortable."

"It will have rats."

I constructed a verbal rendering without rats—an airy space lit by skylights, heated by a ductless heat pump, adorned with built-in cabinets and a private deck. By the time I finished the description, it was nicer than our house. I wanted to live there myself. There was silence on the other end of the line. I knew she didn't have a better solution because I didn't have one.

"I guess we'd better go ahead with this plan."

"For building the apartment?" I said.

"The plan you have for ruining my life."

*

After our inauspicious phone call, it did occur to me that maybe I shouldn't try to move my mother into our house. I didn't discuss the phone call with Nicola, which I knew was a bad sign. Secrets and dishonesty are the gateway drugs of worse behavior. In the end, I justified plunging forward by telling myself it was too late. My mother had agreed to move out, she had nowhere else to go. None of these justifications were really true. We could have pushed to have her stay in her current place for a few more months.

During the 1,250-mile drive from Colorado, I spent some time trying to feel optimistic. When I arrived at her apartment, I discovered that she hadn't packed one single thing. Not even a fork. Since I had last visited her, before we left for Colorado, she had added quite a bit of raw material including an earth-tone La-Z-Boy that had spent most of its life outdoors and what my mother generously called a "love seat," which someone named Hank had helped her drag in from the curb. A rusty bike occupied one corner of the room, accompanied by two suitcases, some tools, and what looked like several trash bags of clothing. I guessed that the bike and tools belonged to the guy named Hank and his cronies who had hauled in the filthy love seat so they could watch movies on my mother's big screen TV, also new. My mother informed me that the TV was probably "hot." We stood looking at each other.

"I thought maybe you would have packed or cleaned a bit," I said. My voice sounded puzzled, not angry. The moment I started to sound angry, things would go downhill fast.

"I did," she said and gestured to the room.

When I looked around the corner, I found mounds of garbage going back to the bedroom. Everything smelled of urine. When I touched a seat cushion, my fingers came back wet. I asked her what was going on, and she said she was having a problem. I shouldn't worry, though, because she was wearing rubber pants now.

"Have you gone to the doctor?"

"You try to find a doctor right now."

I'd forgotten about COVID for the first time since the beginning of the pandemic. She had Medicare and Humana, which came out of her Social Security. "You had a doctor. What happened to your doctor?"

"You're going to really like Hank," my mother said. "He's a fascinating man."

"Please don't tell me he was hit on the head like all the others."

"You have no right to speak that way. Hank has suffered a number of injuries. Not everyone is so lucky, Mr. Fancy Pants."

"Including injuries to his head, right?"

"Yes, but mostly to his back. Otherwise, he would help us move. He lives right over there," my mother said and pointed out the window. I cleaned the pane with the sleeve of my shirt and squinted at a gray apartment building—Section 8 housing for downtown Eugene.

"What floor does he live on?" I asked. If he wasn't too many flights up, maybe my mother could live with him. I had tried to persuade my mother to sign up for Section 8 housing.

"No, he lives in front of the building." There was nothing in front of the building except a rusty, old Ford F-150 with a demolished front end and a self-fashioned tarp home in the truck bed. "He has a generator in there," my mother said and nodded approvingly.

"I bet he does."

It wasn't long, of course, before I met Hank. Reeking of whiskey and not wearing a mask, he stopped by to say how sorry he was that he couldn't help with the move. After he left, my mother watched him limp down the street toward his truck. He pulled back the tarp and crawled in over the tailgate.

"Poor Hank," she said, "someone is going to steal his generator. He's very excited about my moving to your house. He knows the neighborhood very well and loves it up there."

I asked my mother to please take a seat in one of the many chairs and sofas I would have to move on my own. Every time I turned around, there was a new piece of furniture aimed at the TV. Several pieces of luggage, different size shoes, drug paraphernalia—a bong and a bag of needles. Two different TVs, probably stolen, other than the one she'd been using.

"You know," I said, "with COVID, it's not safe to have the whole park population in to watch movies."

"They don't have COVID, they live outside."

"That's not how COVID works."

I tried to add up how long it would take me to disassemble the apartment. Most of it would go to the dump. It would be much saner to hire someone to help me, but I had sailed beyond sane the minute I had set foot in her apartment. I didn't want anyone else involved in what was about to take place over the next few days. I would much prefer to throw out my back and end up in the hospital.

My mother offered me some apple juice, which I declined, though I used the mention of a cold beverage as an opportunity to open the refrigerator door and check on the state of things. As a whirling comet of gangrenous rotten food crashed onto my Muck boots, I leaned over and dry heaved. I had neglected to eat for the last six hours.

"Are you okay?" my mother said.

When I recovered enough to stand upright, I decided to triage the situation and returned to the more important subject of Hank. The man named Hank, I explained to my mother, would not be visiting my house while I was not there. Nicola wouldn't stand for it, and it was her house as much as mine. It wasn't a big house, it wasn't a fancy house, but it was all Nicola and I had. I told her I was setting up cameras in the house that would be connected to my iPhone—not to spy on her, but to make sure everything was *okay*—and that I would know right away if Hank crossed the threshold. I had not planned to set up cameras—the idea had only just occurred to me as I spoke.

As my mother's brow furrowed and her shoulders slumped, I felt my chest tighten with shame.

"You're a monster," she said. "What do you think those people at the university you want to impress would think of what you're saying."

"I have a kid, I have to think of her," I said.

"That's what everyone like you says."

As I moved furniture out to the lawn and bags of trash to the dumpster behind the apartment, she set up one of her kitchen chairs in front of the building. Whether she knew the person or not, every time someone walked up the street while I was carting her stuff, she pointed at me and shouted, "That's my son, the monster!" Several of her neighbors said they hadn't known she was moving. "Off to the gulag! The Stasi have come for me," she told them.

I briefly wondered if I should reverse course and find another solution. As long as she was living somewhere else, in her own apartment, I could step away from her to some extent. If I moved her to our house, she would become more my responsibility than ever. On the other hand, I couldn't leave her in this place. . . . I took eight trips to the dump in the Subaru and, as predicted, strained my back loading the car on the last trip. Whatever she couldn't part with, I moved to our garage for storage, and finally I moved her into what would be Bella's room.

"There," I said, when she emerged from the room to join me in the kitchen. "Isn't this better than where you were?"

She looked out the large windows facing the woods and at the art on our walls.

"Yes, I can die in peace now that I have moved to bourgeoise heaven."

We spent several days in the house discussing how she could shop, where she should walk for exercise. We sat in front of the fireplace and discussed the apartment we would build in the garage. I'd set up an appointment at the doctor. It turned out she had seen another doctor about her incontinence, and he had prescribed medication, which she had refused to take. We went to Walgreens and the grocery store. I had a modest sense that we were gaining control of the situation. Just in case, I bought plastic covers for the bed and a blanket for the sofa.

By the time I was ready to drive back to Colorado, my mother had agreed reluctantly to my conditions: cameras in the living room and kitchen connected to my iPhone, no Hank, no leaving the doors open and wandering around the neighborhood, no messing with the complicated thermostat, which I had set for her on a timer, and she had to collect the mail and bring the garbage out to the garbage cans. If she had trouble with anything around the house, I could call someone to come over and help. She wasn't paying rent. She had a friend who drove a cab who would take her to the grocery store. She said her car was broken, and in any case, it wasn't registered or insured, and she had no license. I had the car towed to the driveway, and she agreed not to drive it.

When I was about to leave, she said, "Jesus, it's like a forced labor camp."

"Except there are no walls keeping you in, no labor to do, you have internet, central heat, an iPad, free Netflix, a fireplace, a stocked fridge, a way to travel around. . . ."

"And no freedom."

I presented the situation to her as I saw it. We'd build her a nice place, she would be in a nice middle-class neighborhood twenty feet from a hundred-acre park, she wouldn't have to worry about all the pesky problems with maintaining an apartment and utilities. I would take care of that, and she would be close to her granddaughter, close to us. We could help her as she got older. She wouldn't be so alone. I told her it was time to come in from the cold. She seemed aware that I was somewhat satisfied with myself.

"It's a good argument," she conceded and scowled at me. "Those are very reasonable points."

When I drove off, I thought we were on decent terms. In other words, I thought I had won. She was in the house, not in the apartment. The garbage was at the dump, not in the house. Near the border between Oregon and Idaho, my phone rang. It was nine thirty at night and I should've been thinking about finding a hotel, but I was keyed up, over-caffeinated, and slightly manic. Nicola was on the phone. She'd been looking after the baby all day long and just wanted to watch her show on Netflix, only the screen was telling her that someone else was using our account.

"I don't understand. If you're driving, who is using our Netflix account?"

"My mother."

"And so it begins. Can you call her and tell her that I just need forty-five minutes of escape before I pass out?"

That seemed reasonable. I pulled the car over on the side of the road (it was sheeting rain now) and clicked on the app on my phone that accessed the cameras in the house. There was my mother sitting peacefully in our living room in front of the fireplace staring down at her iPad. For various reasons, I was reluctant to disturb her. I was feeling mildly triumphant. Here was the image of the mother I had always wanted ensconced in the domestic scene I had worked so hard to create. My mother had always railed against my bourgeois strivings and attachments. As the gap between our circumstances grew, her criticisms had become more acute. She didn't look happy sitting there on the sofa, and I felt ashamed of my immoderate pride in the house, my family, the domestic scene I had wanted growing up.

I didn't want to disturb that image, but at the end of the long road to Colorado was Nicola, who was strung out and tired from watching Bella with no help. I dialed my mother's number.

"I'm right in the middle of watching this movie," she said. "Can I call you back?"

"Actually, I was hoping you could just stop watching for a short time." I explained the situation with Nicola—she just needed a break.

"Are you kidding me?" she said. "This is the most outrageous thing I've ever heard. We all need a *break*. Most of all *me*." She went on to describe what a rough three days it had been. She'd been uprooted, ripped away from "her people."

"Your people? Ripped away?"

"And now that wife of yours is putting the screws to me. It's unbelievable. Also, the thermostat is not working."

"I set the thermostat and asked you not to touch it."

"I was cold. Now it says eighty-two degrees. I've opened the windows."

Nicola was calling again. I put my mother on hold and listened to Nicola tell me how she still couldn't access Netflix. Was there some kind of problem back in Eugene? I told her there was no problem. I just needed a few minutes. I hung up and took a deep breath. It now was sleeting heavily where I had pulled over on the side of the road next to a barbed wire fence. No buildings, cars, or lights for miles.

I logged onto Netflix and upgraded our account for multiple users. I was texting Nicola that she could start watching when a highway patrol car pulled up behind me and the guy knocked on my window to ask if everything was alright. I told him I was sorry—I was just upgrading my Netflix account.

"You're doing what?"

I was halfway into my explanation when I realized he wasn't wearing his raincoat.

"My wife's at home with the baby," I said. "I had to help her out."

"But you're okay?"

There had been a small glitch at home, I told the officer, but I had fixed it.

*

As soon as I arrived back in Colorado, I started to feel more guilty for setting up the cameras in the living room and the kitchen. Nicola joked that I was like the NSA, but I hadn't told her everything about what had happened on my trip to Eugene. If she'd known about Hank and the urine and the state of my mother's apartment, she wouldn't have been joking. Our friends Marjorie and Brian, two of the writers I worked with at the university, thought I was kidding when I told them over the phone. "You set up cameras to spy on your elderly mother?"

I was about to call my mother and tell her to unplug them when I decided I would, just once more, open the app on my phone and see what was going on in the living room. There was a blazing fire with no screen in front of the fireplace. Light from the flames flickered off a large pile of bags, an old rusty bike, and a broken keyboard stacked against the wall. Four candles burned on various wooden bookshelves around the living room, the flames dancing inches away from the books. In the kitchen on camera number 2, a tall, bald man, standing center frame, prepared what looked like an appetizing vegetarian stir fry on our stove. Hank.

My mother appeared on camera number 1 in the living room, settled herself in front of the fire, and put her feet up on the coffee table I had built for Nicola. Hank appeared momentarily with two plates and some silverware. I immediately called my mother. She pulled out her phone, squinted at the number, and set it down on the coffee table. When I called again, she reached over and turned the phone off.

Maybe, I thought, I'm being unreasonable here. They were just having supper. Hank was a friend of my mother's. He was a homeless active alcoholic—I'd known plenty of those—who was looking for a place to crash all winter. Why couldn't I be generous? Maybe what was wrong with me in this case was the same thing that was wrong with the world.

My mother had told me that Hank had options for places to live, all of which required him to stop drinking. He'd stopped drinking many times, according to my mother. He just didn't want to. The question of agency was thorny business with an alcoholic. Hank had been a carpenter, then he hurt his back. That's when the drinking took over. I had asked my mother if Hank wanted to get sober. My mother said he had tried AA and hated it and that he had no interest in life without alcohol. He had stopped for a while on his own and saw no point in living that way. For an alcoholic to even have a chance of staying sober, they had to at least want to stop drinking. I certainly didn't have the whole story on Hank. He had physical issues, with his back, he might have had mental health issues. Now in addition to worrying about my mother, I was worrying about Hank.

I called my AA sponsor in Eugene and talked the whole thing through. He was involved with the Eugene Mission and told me he could get Hank in there for several months. All Hank had to do was at least try to stop drinking.

"What's wrong?" Nicola asked when I came into the living room. Bella was asleep upstairs, and she was sitting by the woodstove sipping tea. I must have looked tense. I told her nothing was wrong as I tucked my phone under my leg.

"There's this guy named Hank," I said eventually, "and he's moved into our house." I confessed everything I had seen in my mother's apartment, everything I knew about Hank. My mother's old friends, the Go Bernies, seemed to have been replaced by the riverside addict community. She'd always been tight with the homeless community wherever she lived and was always trying to help them.

"When were you going to tell me this?" she said.

"I knew I had to tell you," I said. "But I was hoping that after I left . . . she promised not to have him over. I thought it might fix itself."

"Did you hear what you just said?"

"Sort of."

"So now that he knows where we live, all the other people who were hanging out at your mother's apartment know where we live. They'll be over soon."

I nodded. It seemed inevitable.

"Shooting drugs in our daughter's bedroom."

I hadn't thought of it this way, but the answer was yes.

Nicola squinted at me. "We can't have strangers using drugs and getting drunk in our home."

I nodded but at the same time I wasn't sure. It was hard for me to believe that anything really belonged to us. I honestly didn't know what gave me the right to say that I had earned something, that I owned it and someone else didn't. I guessed that this sentiment wouldn't make sense to Nicola. It was *our* home, she might say, we had *worked* for it, and she would be right. We *had* worked for it, but this argument had never convinced my mother. Therefore, it had never really convinced me. My mother had always maintained that the world was structurally unfair, which was undeniable. The world was arranged for the benefit of some people, like me, and not for others, like her. This was also undeniable. So why shouldn't she live in our house and do as she wanted? Why shouldn't the house belong to her? I didn't have any answers.

I called my friend George in Maine to see what he had to say. Halfway into the narrative, he stopped me. *Cameras?* he said and laughed. I told him I didn't think he fully understood the gravity of the situation.

"I understand the situation all right," he said. "Your mother and some late-stage drunk are about to burn your house down."

One of the frustrating things about George was that he usually refrained from telling me what to do.

"You are not the hero of this drama," he said and told me I could call him back later, after our house had burned down.

Out on the porch with my phone, I checked the cameras again—empty except for a mountain of dirty dishes in the kitchen. No one coming or going. I called my neighbor Jamie, who picked up right away. His house, designed by his architect partner, had large glass panels looking out at our dead-end road. I asked him if he had happened to see my mother in her car.

"As a matter of fact," he said, "I just saw her drive away with some bald guy in the passenger seat. I thought you told me that car no longer worked."

"It didn't, or at least I thought it didn't." My mother had lied to me about the car being broken. The car was in my name, but I had removed the insurance because it was not registered and didn't run—so I had thought.

"Seems to work fine," Jamie said, "except it's night and she doesn't have the headlights on."

When I finally got my mother to answer the phone the next day, she said she "completely understood" that she had made a "big mistake." She agreed to walk the keys to her car over to my other neighbor, a former student of mine named Sam. "Because I know you don't trust me," my mother said. Then I wished her happy birthday. In the midst of the chaos, I had almost forgotten.

"I love the present you sent me!" she announced, as if nothing had happened. I had sent her a down jacket so she could go on walks. We chatted about the weather and how nice it was for her to sit by the fire at night. I told her I had spoken to Eric, my AA sponsor in Eugene, about getting Hank into the Mission for a couple months until he could get on his feet. Eric volunteered at the Mission.

"He doesn't want to do that," she said.

"Why not?"

"He wants to live in your house."

At that point I gently returned to the subject of not bringing Hank—or any other active addicts—over to the house.

"Remember," I said, "we talked about this."

"Actually, I'm gonna have to talk to Moose about that one."

"Moose?"

"My therapist. He's training to be a death Doula. Do you have a therapist?"

"What? No. What's a death Doula?"

"You should. *You* are very angry."

She looked at her watch. I could see her looking at her watch on my phone.

"I have to go," she said. "This conversation is over." She hung up and exited stage left.

I waited five minutes and called my neighbor Jamie again.

"Yep," he said. "She just peeled out in the Focus."

A half an hour later she and Hank were back on-screen bobbing around the kitchen making dinner again. Hank did a little jig in front of the camera with a bottle in his hand, gave me the finger, and swatted his fist right at me. His fist was replaced by the message: Video Disabled.

While Nicola helped Bella assemble an octopus puzzle, I reluctantly brought her up to speed on the latest developments. She nodded patiently and responded in a remarkably calm tone.

"So, she's driving around without a license in an uninsured car titled in our name and living in our house with an active alcoholic who has no place to live? And soon there will be a party of others—the same ones who left needles in your mom's apartment—carting off all our things or sleeping in Bella's bed. And this is just Act I of this drama, am I right?"

I hadn't mentioned all the burning candles my mother had set up on the wooden bookshelf.

Nicola stood up and walked over to stand in front of me. Apparently, she wanted to make sure I heard what she was about to say.

"I understand why you had to try this idea out," she said. "But you can't just lift your mother out of her life into our own. Whitebird [an organization that helps the vulnerable in Eugene] can't save your mother, DHS can't save your mother and this guy—what's his name?"

"Hank."

"You can't save them. You've spent your life trying to, and you can't. We've tried to bring her inside the wire, and it's not going to work. Even if you build this apartment on or in the garage with the spare time you don't have—instead of spending time with your daughter—all of this will continue right next to us with Bella there. What does that lead to? You talk about not wanting to repeat the past. In this case, you have to make a choice."

Nicola had understood all along that this wouldn't work, but she had been generous enough to let me run the experiment for myself one last time. I had felt as if I had left my mother behind, alone in a dirty apartment on the other side of town. I didn't want her to live that way, but she was determined to live the way she wanted to live, even if it caused her pain and misery and isolation. I understood that people wanted to make their own decisions and live on their own terms. I'd seen it in AA. Several of the guys I had worked with over the years had died young rather than change. This didn't mean I couldn't help my mother or other people like Hank. It just meant I was no one's savior.

"Now we know," Nicola said. "And we are not going to try this again. Do you understand? If you want to return to Eugene and live with your mother, you can do it without us. Bella and I will come later after you've solved this problem. Not today, obviously, but soon. Before act two."

Nicola wasn't threatening me. She was careful to point that out. She was simply stating that she had limits. The thought of losing Nicola and Bella had never crossed my mind, and I had to sit down on the floor. Nicola was calm and direct, as always, but her eyes were watering. I could see she was serious and upset. The idea that I could rescue my mother and by doing so rescue myself was based on the lie that I could somehow change the past. If I was going to care for my mother as a person, rather than as a character in the drama of my imagination, I had to remember this.

Bella stopped playing with her puzzle and looked at me. In saying no to my mother for the sake of my family, if not myself, I was learning what I had never learned as a child.

I told Nicola she was right.

"I know I'm right," she said without looking away from Bella. "I think it's time to call the police."

"The police?"

I must have looked anguished. Nicola eased up on her outrage and touched my arm. I said I didn't know. I couldn't cut my mother out of my life any more than I wanted her to cut Hank or others out of her life. None of us could afford to cut people off by deciding they were hopeless and didn't matter. Not without inviting the kind of sickness we think we can escape by running away. I had come to see that the question of what role I should play in my mother's life—the question, from one point of view, of what I owed her—was really a question of what we all owed each other. All our troubles begin when we seek to separate ourselves from others, and yet (always a yet) here I was trying to separate my small family from my mother and the chaos we feared.

I tried to explain how I was feeling to Nicola.

"You're not trying to cut her out of our lives," she said. "We're taking steps to make sure they don't destroy our home. Those are two different things."

"But Hank has nowhere to go."

"Is that true? We've talked about this. You talked to your sponsor in Eugene." She was right; Hank could go to the Mission.

"Why don't you call the police and ask them if they're willing to just stop by—nothing violent or extreme. No one's getting dragged out of the house. We only want to nudge your mother and Hank in another direction. I don't think Jamie or Sam are going to be able to get through to her."

In marrying Nicola and having Bella, I had chosen life. Protecting that life, protecting our lives together, had to be the most important thing, but it was no simple thing.

After my mother and Hank finished their supper, I called the Eugene police to at least talk about the situation and see what they said. I explained that Hank shouldn't be in the house and said I did not want him arrested, hauled away, or interfered with in any way. I just wanted them to send a message, if possible, that he shouldn't be there. The officer I spoke to said that they could do that in the mildest way. They were willing to just have a conversation with him, so I said yes.

They showed up a short time later and knocked on the door. My mother shut off the light. She and Hank crouched by the window and tried to peer around the blinds. When the police kept knocking, my mother finally answered the door. The police were kind, they didn't pull Hank out or make threats, but they let him know that he wasn't supposed to be there. I was relieved that I had somehow assuaged Nicola's concerns without hurting anyone—or so I thought.

My mother later told me that the sight of the police had set Hank off. After they left, things unraveled. Hank got drunk and became abusive. In the midst of the ruckus, he destroyed my second camera. He took a piss on our mattress. He threatened to really hurt my mother. She thought he might kill her. He called her names she wouldn't repeat. Names that no one had ever called her before. My mother would never call the police. In her mind, the police were for people who owned property, and she didn't fit into this category. She phoned her cabby friend—a guy who also knew Hank—and the cabby dragged Hank and all his belongings back downtown to his nonfunctional truck.

On the phone the next day I told her I was sorry for setting Hank off by bringing the police into it. I told her if I could go back, I would have found another way. Maybe our neighbor Jamie would have come over.

"Jamie's too nice," my mother said. "And Hank scared me. I didn't know he had that other side to him."

I didn't want to mention her father. "Alcoholics often have that other side," I said.

"I don't understand what it is with me and these alcoholic men. It's like an addiction."

"It's not *like* an addiction," I said. "It *is* one."

"You're so right. I wish you weren't right. But you are."

"You can't save them," I said. "And they can be dangerous. You know that better than I do."

"I'm sorry I drove the car. I don't know what I was thinking. I brought the key over to Sam this morning. He's such a nice man. He and Jamie. He said I could ask him if I ever needed help."

"Listen," I said, "I know things weren't easy when you were young. With your mother and stepfather or with your father—on the farm."

"And it wasn't always easy for you, either," she said.

"But it was worse for you, I know that."

"It was worse for my brothers, I think," she said quickly. "But I don't know."

"The point is that it's no surprise that you find yourself with Hank. I've had similar problems my whole life."

"I didn't know that."

"Yes, I mean not exactly like Hank, but the *wrong* people. Until Nicola. I am sure you remember some of them."

"That married woman with kids."

"Yes, she was one. Many others. The point is that I *understand*. We have to do what we can to help each other. This experiment didn't work out. We'll find another way. We'll find you a good place to live. I'm going to do whatever I can. You know that. You're not alone, so you can relax a bit."

She was silent for a few seconds. "Thank you," she said. "I just don't—I don't know. . . . Sometimes I don't know what I'm doing."

"You don't have to explain."

*

It was sunny and uncharacteristically windless on the morning Bella and I were sitting together on the picnic table in front of the cabin in Colorado while our younger dog, Franny, lay at our feet. Nicola was inside preparing a snack. My wife's mother had recently moved an old horse closer to the cabin, into an area cordoned off with a single strand of electrified tape. The border was only ten feet away, the horse less than twenty feet away, and all three of us, who had no experience with horses, eyed him with anxiety even though he didn't look as if he could move very quickly. Bella edged toward him—she wanted to feed him grass—and I pulled back against her. As Bella cried and tugged harder, Franny rose and looked over her shoulder at me. I'd seen this look before many times over the years since she had joined us as a puppy. I had once thought of this wide-eyed look as a taunt—*try to stop me*, she seemed to say. When the horse took a few steps, Franny turned away from us and shot forward. I bolted to my feet, let go of Bella, and ran after Franny while screaming her name. Caught in the fury of her pursuit, she didn't hear me or couldn't hear me. She lowered to the ground and nipped at the horse's ankle.

Over the previous week, I had been training Franny on leash around the horse. Our other dog, Cheever, kept his distance from the two-thousand-pound animal, but Franny had already charged once, and she had a history of chasing runners, skateboarders, and bikers. She'd learned to tolerate other dogs, even larger dogs like my mother-in-law's eighty-pound lab, so I had thought she would grow accustomed to the horse over time.

I ran after Franny, but it felt as if someone was holding onto my shirt. I couldn't move as fast as I needed to. The horse began to trot as Franny bore down to nip again, and Bella screamed behind me. She had fallen forward when I shot to my feet. The horse stutter-stepped, shifted its weight, and held its hoof in the air. Even at the time, the elegance and coordination of the gesture surprised me—a pro basketball player's miraculous suspension of natural law. The horseshoe hammered into Franny's head so quickly that I didn't see the impact, only heard the cry, indistinguishable from Bella's.

Later, the veterinary surgeon at Colorado State University who tried to save her reassured me that Franny had only done what shepherds do and the horse had done what horses do. But I knew that the people involved—Nicola, my mother-in-law, and most of all me—we had failed because we knew better or should have known better.

When Franny looked at me before chasing the horse, she wasn't taunting me, seeking my permission, or checking to see if she could get away with it. She had been asking me (I now imagined, in her own way, and for her own sake) to stop her from being who she was. As the person, as her person, it was my job to stop her. I had wanted Franny to be herself, to be a dog according to some romantic notion, so I had always given her tacit permission when she looked back. I truly loved to watch her run as much as she loved to tear across a field—but I had always wanted her to come back to me.

The level of grief I felt at Franny's loss took me by surprise. We had lost family pets when I was young, but I couldn't remember feeling this bereft. I felt as if my emotions about Bella, Nicola, my mother, Franny, and my whole life were daisy-chained together. Franny had always jumped up on the bed in the morning when we woke; now Bella started every day asking where Franny had gone. One morning I left to walk by myself. After half an hour, I felt my grief was growing both selfish and distorted and was hardening into a familiar feeling I could only describe as a refusal to accept, not just Franny's death, but everything about the world, including myself.

Weeks passed. We hadn't wanted to leave the cabin since Franny's death, but eventually we ran out of food. Nicola, Bella, Cheever, and I were driving down the seven-mile dirt road to Route 145. The road was wide enough for two cars to squeeze by each other; to the right, the land dropped into a ravine. The road was so steep that I had to put the Subaru in second gear and pump the brakes. As we rounded a sharp corner, a beaten-up Ram truck roared toward us going over forty miles an hour. I quickly pulled over to the edge of the road and stopped with our right wheels less than a foot from the edge of the ravine. As the truck whipped by, I deliberately resisted the temptation to give the guy the finger. I was a father with a toddler, my partner, and a dog in the backseat—not the kind of guy who gave people the finger. The forest service roads around us were used by hunters and ranch workers, most of whom carried guns. I did, however, look up and make eye contact with the guy. This was my mistake. I knew that something passed between us in that split second that he might not be willing to let go.

"Jesus, that was close," Nicola said from behind me as I pulled back onto the road.

A moment later, I looked in the mirror and saw the guy in the truck catching up to us. When he edged to within a foot of our rear bumper, I pulled over into the middle of the road. I didn't want him to pass us—that was my first thought—but I also didn't want him hitting us from behind and sending us into the ravine. As I moved to the side, he sped past us, got in front, and slowed down while weaving until he forced us to stop. His truck was parked at an angle. When he popped open his door, I felt a jolt in my limbs. My vision narrowed, my breath grew shallow. I was undergoing physiological changes whose pathways predated the human species.

The guy wore a fake cowboy hat and had a silver pistol on his belt. He started off yelling at my window. I had no idea what he said as he hit the roof of our car with his fist.

"We have a baby in the car!" Nicola yelled at the guy from behind her window. Bella, who always had something to say, was dead silent. The guy flipped Nicola off and called her a bitch—he held his middle finger in the air as she snapped his picture. Now that she was the focus of his rage, he came fully to life. His eyes dilated, his face flushed. Whatever Nicola represented to him had dredged up hatred in his head. A woman defying him. He was no longer thinking; at this point, neither was I. An image of Franny running after the horse flashed through my thoughts. It felt as if white phosphorous had exploded upward from my chest into my forehead as I unlocked the door, pulled the latch, and started to push my way out. In that moment, I wanted whatever would come next.

"Get back in the car!" Nicola yelled in my ear.

Her voice stopped me. Over our years together, I'd ceded parts of myself to her in the process of becoming the person who now shut the door and locked it.

"Drive," Nicola said. Before I could throw the car in gear, the guy wheeled around in front and pounded on our hood as he continued to yell. I could see the veins in his hand. Nicola and Bella faded into the background. I took my foot off the brake. The car rolled forward a few inches, startling him. The calculation in my head (he was in the way, I couldn't get around him, he had a gun, he was a threat, I was justified) was beside the point. The same white-hot jolt returned, and I wanted to kill him. He was my mother's father. He was me.

He looked me in the eyes for a moment. I don't know what he saw there, but I sensed that he knew the score. He stopped yelling and got out of the way. As I drove past him, he swung his fist into Nicola's window. His knuckles bounced off the glass and we were gone, speeding down the road. When we reached the pavement and had phone reception, Nicola called the Sheriff.

"It's my fault," I said to Nicola, my hands shaking. I was grateful everyone was alive—even the guy from the truck.

"Of course, it isn't," she said. She was shaking, too. "You didn't do anything."

This was not true—I had looked at him as he drove past, which was more than I should've done. There was a part of him in me. He'd seen that. We'd found each other on the road as men had found each other on roads for thousands of years. In another version of this life, I would've gotten out of the car, and I would still be back there with him.

*

In a few months we would return to Eugene, and I would find my mother a place to live downtown, a sunny studio in a vintage building with hardwood floors and all the original fixtures. I had thought it would be impossible to find something affordable, but I did.

My mother would end up liking the idea of the new place—she didn't think it was a "good idea" for her to stay in our house. Living downtown she would be right in the middle of the chaos she couldn't seem to live without. A month after she moved in, a couple of addicts threw tear gas grenades into her building in the middle of the night. In the cold season, wearing more layers than she had in the past, she started collecting blankets from the Salvation Army and walking unsteadily through her neighborhood after dark draping them over people sleeping in doorways. Sometimes she left them food.

These were good days—she spent many afternoons with Bella and me at the dog park and at our house. Bella and I would visit her in her apartment where the two of them would work on art together. In my mind this time seemed to last for decades, though it spanned little more than eighteen months. One night in early January she returned late from a visit to see my sister and her family in New York. She had a cough she couldn't shake, and her apartment was cold. She had bought everyone Christmas presents instead of paying her electricity bill. Nicola and I were in Colorado, and I couldn't reach her because her phone was out of batteries. In the dark, she would have pressed the button on her phone again and again. She was calling to see when I would arrive—she needed some time, maybe ten minutes (which meant twenty-five) to ready herself for our regular trip to the dog park. She should have known I was still in Colorado; she should have known we didn't visit the dog park at night. Her teeth chattered, her hands shook. Her purse was full of special dog treats that she'd hauled all the way from New York under the nose of those TSA people. The dogs always started to howl when they saw her through the window of my truck and licked her face and head as soon as she climbed into the back seat. Where was Jason now?

She stumbled to the bathroom, turned the faucet handle until the water in the tub was as hot as the sun on her face in August, and climbed in still wearing her shirt. Even in Maine, the summer afternoons could be hot. I had promised that I would take her back to visit Maine next summer. Before it was too late, she wanted to see the places on the coast where it had all started—meeting her husband, having a family of her own. If it was possible, if it wasn't too much to ask, she wanted to stand one last time on the shore with her eyes closed and her face raised to the sun as the long exhale of the surf washed over the granite. The salt mist carried the sound of gulls mixed with the voices of her children who would have children of their own. For them, everything might be possible. Her heart stopped as the water rose past the broken top drain, spilled over the lip of the old tub, pooled on the tiles, and spread across the wood floors. On the other side of the country, water inexplicably started spraying from the jets in the tub of my sister's apartment in Brooklyn. Working frantically, my sister and her husband managed to shut off the water and bank towels against the flood, but there was no one on guard at my mother's place. Her studio filled with steam, the light dimmed in the windows. The last sounds to reach her ears would've been the shhhhh of cars plowing through the rain-soaked streets outside and the flow from the tub faucet. No one noticed as the water ran and ran for hours, slipped under the entrance door of her apartment, and poured down one flight of stairs and another to settle in every dip and crevice of the old cellar.

*

When I think of my mother now, I try not to think of her last day when I failed to reach her. I try to think of that time during the pandemic when she was living in our house in Eugene and we were living in Colorado. It still seemed, despite everything, as if the distance between us might close and as if we had many years to repair all that had happened. I could not help but feel that time would wait for us to get it right.

*

One afternoon a month after Hank left our house in a cab, Bella and I were sitting in a window seat I had built on the second floor of the cabin looking over the rolling fields of the mesa toward the San Juan Mountains. A storm was moving in. I called my mother. She was in our house in Eugene and was trying, she reported, to make a fire in the fireplace without the help of Hank. When she asked how things were going in Colorado, I told her about the report from the vet. "I don't know. Bella still wakes every morning calling for Franny."

"She was your dog," my mother said. "Yours and Nicola's and Bella's. Part of your family. And that's the way you and I are about animals. They mean a lot to us. Not everyone is that way about animals. You and I are. We have that in common."

"It's about more than Franny," I said. "I still feel awful."

"That's what it feels like to have so much to lose," she said. "What would it feel like if you had no one?"

"I wouldn't feel anything."

"That's right," she said.

At one time, that's all I had wanted—to feel nothing. Then Nicola and I started our small family—first with each other, then with the dogs, then with Bella. I thought of us all as one unit, protecting each other from the world. Despite my best efforts, my mother remained on the outer edge of our orbit, among those like Hank who had no one to look after them.

Bella stood on the bench seat and leaned her nose against the double-pane glass as Cheever jumped up with us and looked through the window. A purple monsoon cloud sweeping toward us from the west fired bolts of lightning into the mesa.

I asked my mother about Hank. I still felt guilty about terrifying him with the police.

"He's down in his truck," she said. "I check on him sometimes. He can have a place to go inside when he wants to stop drinking for a bit. I spoke to Whitebird, I spoke to Moose."

She asked me, as she did every time we talked, when I would be coming back to Eugene for good. I reminded her how many days remained.

"You don't want to come back, do you?" she said.

I told her it would always be tempting to stay on the mesa surrounded by the natural world. Even if we wanted to, we couldn't afford to remain isolated here, and I doubted Nicola and Bella would want to anyway. Bella especially wanted to be part of the world I was afraid would hurt her someday. I had no idea how to hold Bella close without holding her too close. I didn't always know when I should intercede and try to protect. Sometimes she caught me looking at her, and she would tilt her head and smile. Sometimes leap in the air and spin. I was often astonished by her joy—the joy of a child who was loved and safe—and I felt an immediate bond with all those parents for whom nothing could be more important than watching their children thrive. I knew that parents all over the world and all throughout history had had to watch their children suffer. A single person is nothing in the history of the world, but when that person is your child, then they are the whole universe.

The day would come when Bella would look over her shoulder at me in the same way Franny had. I would try to hold her back, I would call to warn her of the dangers she couldn't see, and she would take off through the grass. I could already feel the thrill and terror of watching her go.

What if, I wondered, everything we would lose and all that would cause us pain was not a threat but rather the very shape of who we were? Our days not empty because they would end and be forgotten but extraordinary because we were here for such a short time. A fair-weather thought, at best, which quickly slipped away.

I pictured the mesa at night. When I let Cheever out to pee before bed, his ears twitched, and he was often reluctant to leave the deck. If I shut off the lights, the sky ignited with distant stars, other worlds, and I imagined the animals around us—mountain lions, bears, elk, and coyotes—wandering among the spindly shadows of aspen groves. For thousands of years, humans had shared parallel lives with all that walked and grew, yet we still didn't understand their language. We barely could communicate with each other.

For a moment I wondered what, if anything, I had to offer anyone outside my own family. People out in the world—in classrooms and AA meetings—didn't need me, but I needed them.

Bella tapped on the window with her finger and said, "Grrr."

"Was that Bella?" my mother asked. "What is she saying?"

Bella tapped on the window again and looked at me. Out on the mesa, just west of us, a large brown bear loped across an open field. The muscles along its back and flank churned under its thick coat. When my mother asked me what was happening, I did my best to describe what we were seeing: the thunderheads approaching, the fourteen-thousand-foot peaks in the distance, the enormous bear traversing the field, probably headed toward the creek.

"You're so lucky you get to see that," my mother said. "Do you know how lucky you are to be there with Bella and to see what you're seeing?" I didn't know how to answer.

Cheever growled at the window and Bella told the bear to "come here right now." She'd never met an animal she didn't want to pat.

The bear stopped before reaching the tree line and looked over its shoulder. Bella's eyes widened. She rested her hand on my back without looking away from the window, and together we waited to see what the bear would do.

Source Acknowledgments

Thanks to the editors of the publications where these essays were first published:

Alaska Quarterly Review: "Animal Stories"

The Best American Essays 2022 (ed. Alexander Chee): "The Wrong Jason Brown"

Florida Review: "A Chest of Drawers"

Harvard Review: "Character Witness"

The New Yorker: "The Wrong Jason Brown"

In the American Lives Series

*The Twenty-Seventh Letter
of the Alphabet: A Memoir*
by Kim Adrian

Fault Line
by Laurie Alberts

Pieces from Life's Crazy Quilt
by Marvin V. Arnett

*Songs from the Black Chair: A
Memoir of Mental Interiors*
by Charles Barber

*This Is Not the Ivy
League: A Memoir*
by Mary Clearman Blew

Body Geographic
by Barrie Jean Borich

*Driving with Dvořák: Essays
on Memory and Identity*
by Fleda Brown

Character Witness: A Memoir
by Jason Brown

Searching for Tamsen Donner
by Gabrielle Burton

Island of Bones: Essays
by Joy Castro

American Lives: A Reader
edited by Alicia Christensen
introduced by Tobias Wolff

*If This Were Fiction: A
Love Story in Essays*
by Jill Christman

*Get Me Through Tomorrow:
A Sister's Memoir of Brain
Injury and Revival*
by Mojie Crigler

*Tell Me about Your Bad Guys:
Fathering in Anxious Times*
by Michael Dowdy

Should I Still Wish: A Memoir
by John W. Evans

*Out of Joint: A Private and
Public Story of Arthritis*
by Mary Felstiner

*Descanso for My Father:
Fragments of a Life*
by Harrison Candelaria
Fletcher

*Homing: Instincts of a
Rustbelt Feminist*
by Sherrie Flick

To order or obtain more information on these or other
University of Nebraska Press titles, visit nebraskapress.unl.edu.